SACRED
SIBLINGS

We are moving toward a world in which the majority of people will be single. In many cultures that time has already come. Yet, our mission environment is most often oriented around married couples. This book surfaces many of the issues that teams will face when members come from these two distinct life situations. As the authors point out in the book, it is easy for us to consider ourselves experts in understanding these challenges. Yet, there is little teaching and writing about this topic. This is a unique resource that readers will find to be relevant in our modern missions era.

TED ESLER
President, Missio Nexus

Sacred Siblings: Valuing One Another for the Great Commission is one of those rare books that tackles an important subject with quantifiable research, together with captivating stories that illustrate key findings in the research. And what a great title—that we all view each other as "sacred siblings"—regardless of marital status. Eenigenburg and Grumelot are not content to just explain the challenges of sacred sibling relationships, of which there are many. They raise the bar and offer the reader much more by sharing practical and actionable suggestions to make these relationships all that God intends for them to be. If you're looking for a very readable and thought-provoking book, this one is for you.

JOHN CERTALIC
Executive Director, Caring for Others

In their book *Sacred Siblings*, Sue Eenigenburg and Suzy Grumelot have brought into focus the need for appropriate perspective of the distinctions and similarities of serving God as a missionary either with or without a spouse and family. This is a useful tool for goers as they can get insight into their own perceptions of their present status and those on the team they will or do work with. It is essential for senders as well, to comprehend the complexities of how those we are trying to care for may struggle or better need encouragement for specific situations and team dynamics. Based off of experience and a realized need, the two gathered information and share it in a meaningful manner. Though there is some anecdotal accounts, they are used in a way in which brings to life how one might feel and thus react to given stimulus from the environment including the team. This makes a great opportunity for the reader to connect similar situations to their own settings. I appreciate this perspective as one needed for any serving in a community of believers where surely there will be a mélange of life situations coming together with a goal to show unity in love—missionary teams and churches both can benefit.

JAMES ARNOLD
Field Director, Serve International—France and Beyond

Sacred Siblings provides us with a compilation of information that goes beyond the anecdotal stories of singles and marrieds serving side-by-side on ministry teams. Through illustrations, not only from Sue and Suzy, but those who participated in the surveys, we get a sense of the challenges, the joys, the disappointments, and the unmet expectations in life together. There are constructive suggestions of ways to serve one another in these sacred extended ministry family relationships. This will be helpful for those who prepare people pre-field, for those who are leading teams along with the couples and singles serving on the teams, and for those who have a ministry of care and consultation for overseas workers. I recommend that after reading it, opportunity is made for dialogue at team retreats and conferences.

FAITH DE LA COUR
Vice President & Chief People Officer, SIM, USA

If you are looking for a book that will help you discover for the first time, or go more in-depth into relationships between singles and marrieds in ministry, *Sacred Siblings* needs to be on your reading list. Sue Eenigenburg and Suzy Grumelot use their years of experience, coupled with survey results, to give the reader a better understanding of the issues, as well as provide practical tools that will help members thrive and be successful in the ministry to which God has called them.

BRETT SHIDELER
VP, Ministry and Care Resources | People Services, Wycliffe Bible Translators USA

Sue and Suzy focus on a particular but critical kind of diversity which exists among those serving in our churches and missions organizations: married couples and singles (and secondarily, men and women). Their research has enabled them to identify areas of life in ministry in which the surveyed marrieds and singles see things differently. In addition to encouraging ministry leaders to be more aware of and consider how to respond to such differences, the authors provide numerous practical suggestions and additional resources to help cultivate better relationships on teams with both married and single members and to increase their effectiveness in the mission.

ERIC SCHLOTTMAN
Leadership Development and Human Resources team,
Cru- Latin America and the Caribbean

Following secular careers, and recently married, God called us into full-time service. As singles, we had supported and volunteered with missions but our expectations were very different from the realities of the challenges ahead! We would have been better prepared if we had read *Sacred Siblings*. Sue and Suzy have given all in ministry a deep and rich treasure chest of biblical and practical tools for understanding one another's needs and examples of how we can be a more loving and Christ-like community. Based on survey responses of married and single workers, they encourage us to ask the difficult questions within our own team/community and examine our assumptions by learning to listen well and communicate effectively.

LYNN AND CHRISTOPHER HOLT
Child Evangelism Fellowship of Europe

"Have you ever seen a majority group, culture, or race that was deeply sensitive to others in the minority? Surely the church should be the place where this is practiced and lived out." (28) Empathy to "feel with" another person and seek to understand their experience, is a powerful tool for helping us to work together effectively. Often we study and seek to understand the people group we are trying to reach, their felt needs, concepts of God, etc., but we often miss taking time to hear the stories and hearts of our brothers and sisters serving beside us. When seeking to make organizational decisions, experiencing conflict or considering challenges, this gap can cause us to make assumptions, devalue our colleagues, or keep us from functioning as effectively as we could together. *Sacred Siblings* compiles many of these stories for us to peer inside others' experiences, gives us questions to ask one another, and very practical tips for engaging and partnering together effectively.

RACHEL HEFFIELD, PHD
PCC-SThriving Catalyst-VP Member Development, Pioneers

As an MK, my missionary parents invited a single colleague to become a part of our family. Later, as a global worker, my husband and I often had our single co-workers in our home. Sue and Suzy's book opened my eyes to how poorly I may have served them due to my assumptions that I knew the needs of my single friends. Now as I work in member care, I am convinced this book is greatly needed to help our teams function as the body of Christ, loving each other as brother and sister. While I often threw around that phrase, I really didn't know what it meant. This book gives me practical suggestions for how I can make that a reality.

EVA BURKHOLDER
Christar

Thank you, Sue and Suzy, for this much needed tool which can help us married men realize how we may be unconsciously treating the women in our mission, in particular our single women, especially when it comes to mission leadership. But this book is not just about how married men should treat single women, it is about how believers of both genders and any marital status should treat one another. We all have blind spots, but our perceptions as to how we are treating others is one where we don't need added surprises. Throughout this book, Sue and Suzy provide us with examples from their lives and ministries which illustrate the principles they are discussing. Added to this are well-written discussion questions which can help us grow in these areas and which can be used for group discussions. It is my opinion that this is a book that should be read by all mission leaders and especially those who are involved with member care.

DR. JAMES CARLSON
Director, International Church Initiatives
Evangelical Free Church of America, ReachGlobal Europe

Sue Eenigenburg and Suzy Grumelot have given the Body of Christ a good gift by providing us the tools to identify misunderstandings between married folks and singles and by offering us the resources to build relational bridges between the two groups.

LEWIE CLARK
Director, Icon Ministries, Chicago

As a single missionary who has been the only single on two teams, I greatly appreciate the work Sue and Suzy have done to identify misunderstandings between marrieds and singles that create obstacles to healthy, thriving teams. I can identify with the frustrations my single brothers and sisters shared, and I learned valuable things about how to work well with married colleagues. I would recommend this book as required reading for all missionaries—married and single, new to the field and veterans—and pray God will use it to help us serve more effectively in the fields where He has sent us.

CHERY FLORES
Missionary, Mission to the World (MTW)
Women's Ministry Coordinator, MTW Europe

Since the vast majority of our "single" missionaries work in a team environment I found Sue and Suzy's work to be very intriguing. Most helpful, to me, was the undeniable fact that expectations, both real or perceived, differ greatly between the married and single missionary. What a great tool Sue and Suzy have provided both parties to help navigate these often tricky relationships and ultimately promote the growth of the Kingdom through highly functioning missionary teams. I would recommend this book to any missionary, single or married, working in a team environment.

BRIAN GARRISON
Associate Mission Director, Baptist Bible Fellowship International,
World Mission Service Center

As a member care provider, I hear from single and married missionaries alike who feel misunderstood by their teammates. Teams will benefit from discussing the themes of *Sacred Siblings*. The stories of the authors and other missionaries will validate the experiences of individual readers and cause them to consider more carefully the experiences of others. I will recommend this book to missionaries I work with.

K. H.
Avant Ministries

Single men and women continue to make significant contributions to global missions. *Sacred Siblings* addresses the importance of understanding one another as singles and marrieds work together for the sake of the Kingdom. Through careful research, Sue and Suzy provide practical suggestions for healthy working relationships, bringing greater value to our single colleagues!

DOROTHY JANZEN
SEND

Singles and married people serving together on ministry teams show a significant strength of God's design, but they are often a recipe for conflict and misunderstandings! *Sacred Siblings* will be an excellent resource to any ministry team with the desire to love and serve each other better, bringing glory to God!

TAMMY LUNDELL
One Challenge International (Europe area leadership)

I believe this book is an important contribution to the body of literature in field of ministry team dynamics, and specifically with regard to the challenges faced by marrieds and singles serving together in mission. The authors have presented and explained a great deal of essential information in a way that is approachable and understandable, and have offered practical suggestions for overcoming or mitigating the challenges that have been identified. I thoroughly enjoyed the book, and I believe it should inform discussions and policies throughout the mission community in the years to come.

DR. ROBERT LUGAR
One Another Ministries Int'l

Suzy and Sue show us our divergent perspectives as single and married team members and ask us to carefully reflect on several powerful questions as we serve together. We are truly sent to be ambassadors for Christ and to bring transformation; as we do, our Savior needs to be supremely evident in our relationships with one another. I'm grateful for their work in providing tangible steps for each of us to grow more in the image of Christ.

BRENT MCHUGH
International Director, Christar International

A key point in the book is that whether you are married or single, people tend to see the best in each other's world, but that is not the sum of a married or single person's life. From the research shared in the book, we have an opportunity to hear the other side of life as it relates to married and single people. As we listen with an empathetic ear to the hurts and challenges faced by our brothers and sisters, we learn to move forward together to accomplish the Great Commission. I encourage you to read on this important and timely topic for the glory of God.

KIM MCHUGH
Christar International

Relationships are more of a journey than a single moment. Ministry team relationships are especially susceptible to the bruises and pains of "missing one another" when assumptions are made about others or expectations go unmet from the team. Suzy & Sue provide us with a much needed framework for slowly and deliberately addressing the relational necessities of each team member, so that the team, community, and mission organization can more fully reflect the fullness of the Body of Christ. These are two sisters in whom I have great trust, and I commend this book to you, your team, or your organization.

DAVID RIDDELL
International Director, World Team

It's not a surprise that issues—such as unmet expectations, misunderstandings, unintentional oversights, and break-down of trust on teams—are prevalent in missions. What is amazingly simple is that all these issues can be used to produce growth if communication improves. We can all learn to be better LISTENERS, which is a huge step in the right direction toward healing and maturing in Christ. Sue and Suzy have put a finger on these issues that are often overlooked because of their simplicity, and they give us great suggestions for ideas about how to move forward in healthy relationships. As they examine assumptions, expectations, and communication obstacles that exist between singles and marrieds, we quickly see that the principles can be applied to just about any relationship.

PAUL MUSSER
One Collective (formerly International Teams (ITeams)

To navigate team relationships well requires intentional effort and constant attention. It also demands knowledge of the various dynamics that are involved. Sue Eenigenburg and Suzy Grumelot have done us the favor of digging through most every relationship one can experience in missions, guiding us to an awareness of what is often missed. Sue, a long-term married missionary and Suzy, a long-term missionary single blend their individual experiences resulting in a comprehensive understanding of missionary relationships that is second to none.

MARVIN J. NEWELL
Senior VP, MissioNexus

Having spent my first ten years as a single in the military and Christian Service I appreciate this work on the value of relationships. *Sacred Siblings* conveys relational, personal and cultural insights on the greatness of God's family, Psalm 68:5–6a.

DAN PAINTER
Founder/Pres Emeritus, International Christian Community—Eurasia

With careful interpretation of survey data, Sue Eenigenburg and Suzy Grumelot present practical suggestions for teams to live out the theology of family. That is, to live as sacred siblings—brothers and sisters in Christ who model Christ-like love, seeking to understand and to honor each other whether single, married, male, or female.

MARILYNN PLUCAR
ReachGlobal Member Care Co-Director

In this easy to read handbook, Sue Eenigenburg and Suzy Grumelot have provided a statistically validated window to see clearly some key differences between how singles and marrieds experience working together on assignment. This is an excellent resource and should be required reading for teams working together both on and off the field.

BARRY DANYLAK PHD
Author of *Redeeming Singleness: How the Storyline of Scripture Affirms the Single Life.*

Perspective, insight and understanding—this book is invaluable in aiding wise leadership and effective ministry. A unique research based understanding is offered of how faithful single and married servants of God see things differently, leading to misunderstanding and dysfunction in teams—even in teams where each member genuinely longs for God's Glory in the nations through their fellowship in the Gospel. The practical suggestions which flow out of the research and experience of the writers will help diverse teams flourish in accomplishing their missional calling.

HARRY ROBINSON
Executive Director, One Another Ministries International

I was so drawn into this topic and your manuscript that I have sat on the side of my bed for hours tonight reading what you sent to me. Singles and married people and their children are all critical partners in missions. There are inevitable tensions there which must be dealt with biblically, sensitively and regularly. If God truly does have plans for us (for good … to give us a future and hope) then is single life better and more productive or is married life better? I say, let God write our story.

STEVE SAINT
founder of ITEC, author of three books, and son of Nate Saint

These ladies share valuable insight, stemming from years of experience working through these very issues every cross-cultural worker faces with team dynamics. They will help you understand the value of a team and how to recognize the gifts each person can contribute towards building a healthy team that can grow stronger together.

NICKI SMITH

This is an excellent book about team relationships. Sharing how relationships matter, and are complicated, complex, and demand commitment Tackling the challenges of communication, listening well, knowing each others expectations, and the danger of assumptions in relationships are covered so well, with both information gathered from surveys, and their shared personal experiences. This is a book to learn from, be encouraged by, and share what you learn with your teammates, as well as a tool that will bring a greater understanding of who we are as individuals, and how we all are made to give glory to God.

HEATHER SHOTTON
WEC, UK

The authors of *Sacred Siblings* present relevant issues in the mission community which have begged to be addressed for a long time. Their research reveals significant disparity in perspectives of singles (male and female) and marrieds, and even touches on male and female misunderstandings of need for community. The creative and innovative suggestions offered by survey respondents and the authors are practical, allowing for individuality, without requiring uniformity. Well worth the attention of mission leadership and constituents alike!

MARTI WILLIAMS
Director of Diversity and Women's Initiatives, TEAM

By naming "un-named" dynamics that run our relationships, this book gives important insight for embracing greater potential to be enriched personally and professionally, as well as better expressing the heart of as the people of God. Living and relating by assumptions and expectations is a path to diminished personhood. We all do it, and suffer for it! But we can learn to see each other as the multi-faceted adults that we are. In *Sacred Siblings*, you'll find biblical perspectives and strong stories that unpack them! Traits such as single/married, male/female, introvert/extrovert only describe one aspect of who we are, so to consider how much weight a category bears in the way we think about someone is a good, stretching exercise that unleashes helpful perspectives to propel us out of our self-centric ruts—making us better people and so better missionaries. I'm grateful to have this important resource about learning to be the diverse, spiritual people of God that are building His Kingdom, and not defining the Body of Christ by anything less!

WENDY WILSON
Executive Director, Women's Development Track—Missio Nexus Mission

Married or single, we often see each other living in "greener pastures." Relationships can be complicated but God made us inter-relational, and has gifted each person to make a unique contribution to the ministry team we serve with. *Sacred Siblings* helps us to better understand one another and provides many practical suggestions to navigate through the relational dynamics between singles and married people in a loving way. A must read for anyone on a team or those who care for and support global kingdom workers.

N. YOUNG
Singles in Community Lead, SIM International

Sue Eenigenburg & Suzy Grumelot

SACRED SIBLINGS

WILLIAM
CAREY
PUBLISHING
Available at missionbooks.org

Valuing One Another for the Great Commission

Sacred Siblings: Valuing One Another for the Great Commission

Published by William Carey Publishing
10 W. Dry Creek Cir
Littleton, CO 80120 | www.missionbooks.org

William Carey Publishing is a ministry of Frontier Ventures
Pasadena, CA 91104 | www.frontierventures.org

Mike Riester, Pam Fogle, interior design
Mike Riester, cover design
Beverly Guy and Andrew Sloan, copyeditors
Melissa Hicks, managing editor

ISBN's: 978-1-64508-216-3 (paperback), 978-1-64508-218-7 (mobi),
978-1-64508-219-4 (epub)

Printed Worldwide
23 22 21 20   2 3 4 5   IN

Library of Congress Control Number:2019945857

To our brothers and sisters in Christ
laboring side-by-side
in the world
for the glory
of God

Contents

Foreword

RELATIONSHIPS ARE COMPLICATED. If you doubt that, then become a missionary! The arena of missions is full of relationships—everywhere and all the time. Not a single day goes by that you don't interact with somebody. After all, that is what missions is all about—being God's messenger to hurting, broken people. If it were otherwise, God would have commanded the angels to reach lost humankind. But he didn't. Instead he commissioned you and me to reach other human hearts.

Missionaries are to be doing just that, though it puts them squarely in the place of complicated relationships they would not have experienced otherwise. Interpersonal relationships on all levels are compounded when one ministers cross-culturally. It comes with the territory.

Relationships are complex. If you doubt that, then become a missionary! Just a few weeks into the work will have you amazed at the complexity of relationships with teammates. At times you will scratch your head and wonder how and why you were paired with some of those on your team. Other times you will be so grateful for those same coworkers who came to your aid and bailed you out of a trying or difficult circumstance. Team relationships can be messy, trying, unbearable, sweet, fulfilling, and rewarding all at the same time.

To navigate team relationships well requires intentional effort and constant attention. It also demands knowledge of the various dynamics that are involved. Sue Eenigenburg and Suzy Grumelot have done us the favor of digging through most every relationship one can experience, guiding us to an awareness of what is often missed. The genius of this book is that one author, Sue, has been a long-term married missionary and the other, Suzy, a long-term single missionary. The blending of their individual experiences results in a comprehensive understanding of missionary relationships that is second to none.

Rooted in professional research, the authors give strong credence to what they have to say. They have looked at missionary relationships from every possible angle. As I read through the multiple topics they cover, at times I felt affirmed with my on-field experiences; other times I felt very convicted—to the point of sadly wondering how many coworkers I blindly and unintentionally offended. No doubt you will feel the same as you read.

In the book of Ecclesiastes, Solomon tells us that "Two are better than one" (Eccl 4:9). That is so true in mission work. Being on a team may be harder, but it is better. The apostle Paul knew that, and that is why his teammates—up to seven at one point—are mentioned by name in Acts 20:4. But it is interesting to note that, soon after, Paul does something that is not recorded elsewhere. He takes a couple of days to get alone by walking solo from Troas to Assos, telling his team to take the boat (Acts 20:13–14). Paul, the master team leader, who believed in and built up his own team, needed some solitary time. Yes, even Paul knew that relationships are both complicated and complex.

Relationships demand commitment. If you doubt that, then become a missionary! Loyalty, devotion, allegiance, and steadfastness are demanded in relationships. This is true not only on the human level but in relation to the divine as well. The authors conclude this book with the reminder that whatever the pains of separation—and in missionary life there are many—they pale in comparison to the worthiness of Jesus and the glory that is to come. So if you are currently a missionary, stay the course. If you are in a trying relationship with coworkers, national believers, mission administrators, or your home church, don't bale out—work it out. This book was written to guide you through that process.

MARVIN J. NEWELL
Senior Vice President, Missio Nexus

Acknowledgments

WE ARE GRATEFUL FOR THE WORK of Sue Edwards, Kelley Mathews, and Henry J. Rogers in their book *Mixed Ministry: Working Together as Brothers and Sisters in an Oversexed Society.* Their words "sacred siblings" captured this holy family relationship we have as men and women in the family of God. It is an honor to use their phrase as the title for our book.

We want to thank our mission agencies, Christar and World Team, for their care for us through the years. Together, Suzy and I have sixty-three years of cross-cultural ministry experience! Our agencies' leadership has encouraged us to use our giftings for the glory of Jesus at home and abroad.

We are deeply grateful to the mission agencies who passed along our survey to their members. We thank God for the men and women who invested their valuable time in completing this survey. Your efforts to communicate strengths, needs, and ideas for single and married missionaries have been beneficial. Your voices were heard. Readers will learn from your insights and stories.

We are grateful to Rosanna Hess, whose expertise in analyzing data has been foundational in documenting and understanding this research! Kim, Jayme, Hadassah, Liz, Robert, Eva, Karla, Nicki, and Marv all reviewed the rough draft to help us refine our writing! Bev Guy did an excellent job editing our manuscript.

One Another Ministries hosted us for our week of working on the rough draft of this book. For over thirty years One Another Ministries has provided services to hundreds of organizations, churches, and sending agencies, as well as thousands of international Christian workers of over one hundred nationalities serving in more than 140 countries around the world—often during the most difficult times of their lives.

Shoulder to Shoulder is an initiative of One Another Ministries. Its efforts have focused on empowering, equipping, and encouraging single missionaries and those who serve with them. Their services range from retreats to consultations, from personal interviews to gatherings for international leaders. We are grateful that through one of their training programs we could meet each other and be encouraged to produce this material.

I (Sue) want to thank my husband, Don, for his encouragement to write, travel, and research new topics. I have learned many important life lessons from my children. I am grateful to God for his work in their lives and for the beautiful gift of seeing his grace and faithfulness extending to the next generation.

I'm thankful for my parents and their care for me for over sixty years! They have modeled love, and they continue to keep me stocked in Reese's Cups!

I appreciate my team, who has cheered me on with jingle pen celebrations. I've appreciated Suzy's expertise and willingness to share her story as a single woman called by God to serve him. It was a privilege to visit the church she helped plant in Paris and witness her love for people and her host country.

I (Suzy) want to thank my physical family, who has stood so faithfully behind me all these years. My parents, my siblings and their spouses, and my nieces, nephews and "greats" bring joy across the miles. I appreciate my spiritual family, which includes all the supporters and friends who have regularly prayed for me and for this writing project. My French brothers and sisters, along with my World Team missionary colleagues, have also encouraged me to press on in this journey. I often say I couldn't do what I do without the care, friendship, and regular "lifting before the throne of grace" of so many. You know who you are! Merci beaucoup!

I'm also grateful for Barry Danylak, whose life and work have impacted my life so powerfully and largely influenced this book. Anne Depret on the Isle of Groix and Colleen Sumner on Vancouver Island have mentored, prayed, and fasted through the whole process. Dianne Becker and Sandy Jeffers encouraged me to say yes to writing, as did Dorcas Harbin, Margaret Hadley, and Cathy Thompson. The rest of the One Another Ministries/Shoulder to Shoulder team has cheered us on too. Thanks, Twala, Harry, Robert, and Deb.

It's been a joy to get to know Sue and Don and hear a bit more of their long trek of faithfulness in many desert places. I admire Sue's wit, grit, and gift of writing. I appreciate most her intimate walk with Jesus and her friendship. I have fond memories of a working visit in Spain, meeting her (and Don's) teammates at Christar and enjoying sweet fellowship in their apartment. Thanks for introducing me to tea with churros and chocolate in Málaga!

Preface

WHEN A BOOK IS WRITTEN BY TWO AUTHORS, it can be confusing to know who is writing what. To help clarify, throughout the book Sue is the primary author and it will be noted when it is Suzy's story or perspective.

The two introductions lay the foundation for why we began this research, how we did the research, and the results of that research. After that the book is divided into the issues reflected by the significant differences in the opinions of married and single missionaries.

In the first section, we look at areas in which significantly more married people thought certain statements were true than their single coworkers. This section can be broken into five major parts: value, training, communication, relationships, and contentment.

The second section deals with areas in which significantly more single people thought certain statements were true than their married coworkers. All four chapters in this section focus on the expectations of single missionaries—expectations in regard to community, being seen as mature, receiving practical help from teammates, and ministry involvement.

Also mentioned throughout these two sections are some significant differences between the perspectives of men and women, as well as between married women and single women. Of course, the differences in these perspectives affect us throughout our organizations and especially on teams that work more closely together.

Though ideas and possible solutions can be found throughout these sections, each chapter will conclude with what we consider to be some good ideas, helpful tools, and an application question.

We close the book in section three with a challenge to release more workers for the kingdom. As sons and daughters, parents and grandparents, we must respond when God calls and bless those who go. Married or single, when God calls us may we answer like Isaiah: "Here am I. Send me!" (Isa 6:8). And when God calls our children, may we say, like Hannah: "I prayed for this child, and the LORD has granted me what I asked of him. So now I give him to the LORD. For his whole life he will be given over to the LORD" (1 Sam 1:27–28).

INTRODUCTION 1

The Who and Why

Sue

I FIRST MET DON WHEN I WAS A STUDENT at Moody Bible Institute. We met at the gym—not the huge facility they have now, where teams that are in town to play the Chicago Bulls practice, but a little gym called North Hall. I went with a group of girls to play volleyball. He went with a group of guys to play basketball. The girls got there first, so the guys joined us in a game of volleyball. Due to the size of the gym, only one sport could be played at a time!

After we finished playing volleyball, some of us decided to stay to play basketball. Having played on a team in high school, I had quite a nice outside jump shot. Don noticed that about me.

There were three things I noticed about Don. One, he passed the ball to girls. This was not a normal thing in the 1970s. Guys assumed girls couldn't play well, so they would often hog the ball. I was impressed. Second, he never lost his temper. Winning or losing, he was calm, cool, and collected. I was very impressed. The third thing I noticed—and though I mention this last, it was the first thing I noticed—was that he had great legs! Not since watching Carlton Fisk play baseball had I admired a man's legs this much. I was thoroughly impressed.

After returning to my room, I looked Don up in the yearbook. I had no clue how to begin to say his last name! It turns out he was also in my church history class. And he sat next to me the following semester in theology class. We had deep theological discussions on the way to chapel. If I could come up with a hard enough question, our discussion lasted so long that we ended up sitting together.

Soon we started dating. Around the same time, I was reading 1 Corinthians and came to chapter 7:

> I would like you to be free from concern. An unmarried man is concerned about the Lord's affairs—how he can please the Lord. But a married man is concerned about the affairs of this world—how he can please his wife—and his interests are divided. An unmarried woman or virgin is concerned about the Lord's affairs: Her aim is to be devoted to the Lord in both body and spirit. But a married woman is concerned about the affairs of this world—

how she can please her husband. I am saying this for your own good, not to restrict you, but that you may live in a right way in undivided devotion to the Lord. (1 Cor 7:32-35)

Jesus had changed my life. I wanted to serve him wholeheartedly and unreservedly. After reading this passage, I saw marriage as an obstacle to my service to the Lord. I did not want to be divided in my devotion to God. But I still liked Don.

As our relationship progressed, we often had long talks about marriage. I struggled with seeing marriage as an option if it was going to limit my walk with God and my ministry for him. I also struggled because I was growing in my love and respect for Don, his heart for the Lord, and his desire to serve him. If I was convinced about being single and doubtful about marriage, why was I dating him?

Don had three older brothers who were married and involved in ministry with their wives. And I grew up watching couples who served God together. It didn't seem like marriage was a hindrance to them. There was also the passage in Ephesians 5 that talked about marriage reflecting the love of Christ for the church and the church's submission to him.

Submit to one another out of reverence for Christ.

Wives, submit yourselves to your own husbands as you do to the Lord. For the husband is the head of the wife as Christ is the head of the church, his body, of which he is the Savior. Now as the church submits to Christ, so also wives should submit to their husbands in everything.

Husbands, love your wives, just as Christ loved the church and gave himself up for her to make her holy, cleansing her by the washing with water through the word, and to present her to himself as a radiant church, without stain or wrinkle or any other blemish, but holy and blameless. In this same way, husbands ought to love their wives as their own bodies. He who loves his wife loves himself. After all, no one ever hated their own body, but they feed and care for their body, just as Christ does the church—for we are members of his body. "For this reason a man will leave his father and mother and be united to his wife, and the two will become one flesh." This is a profound mystery—but I am talking about Christ and the church. However, each one of you also must love his wife as he loves himself, and the wife must respect her husband. (Eph 5:21-33)

At first, I thought that staying single would be the more spiritual thing to do; it would bring more honor to the Lord to serve him without distraction. Then, as I thought about marriage, I saw that married people too could be used by God as they served him separately but also together. Each person has a calling from God. Some are called single; some are called married. The important thing is to respond to that call of God through prayer, by faith, and in full obedience.

As Don and I sought God together and prayed about it, I came to understand that we could serve God together as a married couple. And so we have in our forty-plus years together. As God's children, as spouses, as parents, as missionaries, we have sought to follow God's call on our lives to serve him. Together we've moved about fifteen times and lived on four different continents. We've raised four children we love. There were tears along the way—theirs and ours! There were hugs, kisses, misunderstandings, mistakes, wins, losses, and always—by God's kindness and power—an abiding, underlying love through it all. We have now gained four more adult children we also love, and with them God has blessed us with twelve grandchildren we adore.

We've had many different roles in ministry. We've served on various teams, with both married and single brothers and sisters. Each one has enriched our lives, for which we are truly grateful. A married friend encouraged me to "get it fixed" when I was angry with Don. Some single friends saw that we were stressed and offered a weekend of babysitting so that we could get away. My children had "aunts and uncles" on our team who prayed for them. These non-blood relatives modeled living by faith so our kids could see what that looked like, whether married or single. Our teammates invested in their lives and in ours.

I am grateful for God's leading. I am thankful for my husband. It is an honor for me to serve the Lord. I know how cross-cultural ministry has been as a married woman. I don't have a clue what it would be like as a single. From what I've learned in this research, one of the biggest mistakes married missionaries make is assuming we know how it is because we've been single ourselves. But I have never been a single missionary. I humbly admit that I don't know what it's like. I've known single missionaries. We've talked. I've listened and observed. I have ideas. But I do not know.

Margaret Clarkson talks about this in *So You're Single:*

> Because married people were all single once, they tend to think
> that they know all there is to know about singleness. I suggest
> that this is not so; that there is a vast difference between being
> single at 25 or 30, with marriage still a viable possibility, and being
> single at 45 or 50 or 60, with little or no prospect of ever being
> anything else. Singleness has a cumulative effect on the human
> spirit which is entirely different at 50 than at 30. (1978, 10)

It goes both ways.

A single woman who was on our first team contacted me several years ago. She had gotten married, and she and her husband had four children. She wanted me to know that if she ever gave the impression that she thought I didn't do enough ministry outside of that which took place in our home, she apologized. She now understood more of where I was coming from and how I invested my time. I don't remember ever feeling judged by her, but she must have had some concerns about my ministry based upon her apology. We had talked together. She had listened and observed. She had ideas. But she did not know.

The primary reason for this book is to give married and single people working together on teams a clearer understanding of what each other is thinking, feeling, and experiencing. The data gives us a place to begin dialogue about critical issues we face when working together. It is OK to say we don't know. It is more than OK to ask each other questions so we can learn from each other. Assumptions kill team relationships. Listening to each other brings life.

Another reason for this book is to help mission organizations better assess areas of strength and weakness when it comes to preparing married and single people to work together on teams. Organizational leaders can learn what communicates value and what training could be useful. This research gives them a chance to hear what single and married cross-cultural workers are saying about their relationships with each other and their organizations.

The final reason I will mention is to honor both single and married persons called by God to serve him across cultures by sharing their stories, opinions, challenges, and joys. Our marital status does not define us; it does not give us fulfillment or maturity. God delights in each of his children, and he writes a story in each of our lives—using our different strengths, personalities, and marital statuses—in which he is the hero.

May he use each of us for his glory.

Suzy

IN THE SUMMER OF 1982, God started opening my heart to the great needs in Europe and the broader cross-cultural mission field. I was working with World Team in their international headquarters in Coral Gables, Florida. In that role I spent a couple weeks helping with a conference for missionaries, and later I visited Italy and France. The great spiritual needs and the lostness around me impacted me deeply, and I began to wonder if God might be calling me into these harvest fields.

As I was leaving France, I shared this with a wise missionary friend. She urged me to make certain of the calling, saying she had seen many come and go. Then she explained, "A deep sense of call is the only thing that will keep you here when times are tough." She impressed upon me the importance of making sure. So I returned to Florida telling the Lord that I would do nothing unless he made it crystal clear. That's when the wrestling with God began and when he did indeed issue a call into cross-cultural missions.

One of the people God used to confirm that call was the singer/songwriter Keith Green. I had not been a fan of Keith's music, but I was enjoying his Songs for the Shepherd album that summer. That led me to receive the Last Days Newsletter in my mailbox at just the moment I was asking God to speak. Keith, along with two of his children and another family in their ministry, had been killed in a plane crash. This September/October 1982 newsletter, no longer in print, discussed the call to serve in missions and it was the last message Keith wrote, just days before the tragic accident. The articles were later adapted as "Why YOU should go to the Mission Field."

In that article, Keith discussed the call of all believers to go and make disciples, and how each of us need to figure out our role and place in obeying this call. He went on to write about the most common excuses for not going to the mission field. I don't remember what many of the excuses were, but I know that the two that were holding me back from saying yes were on the list. First, I didn't want to have to raise support; and second, I didn't want to go alone.

Regarding support—well, I didn't even like selling Girl Scout Cookies, and I hated the idea of asking for money. Keith went on to talk about how God's call comes complete with all the equipping and resources needed to fulfill all he asks of us. And he explained that if God is calling us, it's up to him to provide. Suddenly I understood that it wasn't me who had to raise the support, but God. That took a huge burden off my shoulders and removed that hurdle in answering the call.

But my second concern still gave me great pause. You see, I felt called to be a missionary wife, but there was no husband on the horizon! Somehow it felt like a much bigger commitment to strike out on my own than to go with a God-given partner. In that article, Keith pointed out something that I hadn't thought about before. He argued that marital status was a secondary issue, and that the most critical issue was finding God's will for our lives and doing it. He also said that the best place to find the person God had for me—if indeed God had a future spouse as part of his perfect plan for my life—was in the center of his will. That made so much sense and removed my last hurdle to answering that call. That was thirty-five years ago!

God did provide all my support in amazing ways, and he has continued to provide for all my needs these past thirty years as a church planter in France. I'm still waiting for that partner in ministry, but I have no doubt this single journey has been part of his plan. Along the way I've learned a lot more about God and about his provision and about sufficiency in Christ. I've always believed that while marriage offers daily opportunities to practice grace and forgiveness, singleness offers daily opportunities to practice dependence and trust. And all of us must answer the question, "Is God really enough?"

In 2001, I had the opportunity to spend some time with a team of missionaries in Ireland. One of the leaders was sharing about sacrifice. He went on to say that very few things in life are worth a great price. He finished by saying, "Surely the cause of Christ is one of them, worthy of great sacrifice." Yes, my heart agreed! That gave me peace to give God my unchosen singleness. I always say that I never wanted to become a poster child for single missionaries, but it's sort of happened over the years.

In 2004, I was asked to speak at a mission conference at Tabor College Victoria (now Eastern College Australia). After I accepted, I was asked to add a session with the student body addressing the issue of singleness in missions. I remember thinking that I had nothing to say on the subject. And as I prepared my talk, I discovered that there were hardly any resources on the subject. In the end, I felt I had more questions than answers. So I shared the things that troubled me: how the church and the missions world handled this subject in light of Scripture. I shared some of the challenges and unhelpful messages I'd heard, but also the conviction that God was in this journey and calling. Again, I felt I'd raised more questions than I'd answered. I left the students with the meager resources I'd discovered and urged them to let me know if they came across better ones.

Fast-forward to May 2, 2007, when I felt that God finally began to give me some powerful answers. The director of training for World Team, Chuck Sutton, sent me a link to a sermon that John Piper had just preached, entitled "Better Than Sons and Daughters." This was the first sermon I'd ever heard that affirmed and validated me as a single person in the body of Christ. His message brought together things I knew and sensed but had never heard from the pulpit or in training as a church planter.

Piper kept referring to "A Biblical-Theological Perspective on Singleness," written by Cambridge scholar Barry Danylak, as the inspiration for his sermon. I just had to get my hands on the original document that had so spoken to Piper. I had never Googled anything before, but I was desperate. I couldn't find the actual document, but my Googling took me to the author and even gave me his email address. I was convinced this was a cyber mistake and something I shouldn't be able to get, but I went ahead and wrote to this stranger, asking if I could read the broader work that had influenced Piper's then week-old sermon.

To my surprise, Mr. Danylak wrote me back, giving me the link to the twenty-page document he wrote just before starting his doctoral studies in Paul's discussion of singleness in 1 Corinthians 7. As I read through it, I felt like I had gold in my hands. Here were the answers to so many of my questions. It had huge implications for me, but also for the church in general and the churches we were planting. I ended up passing along that document all around the world—including to some of those people I'd shared with in Australia. I later wondered if this work spoke so deeply to me just because I was single, but I sensed it was something bigger and included some core gospel truths that had gotten lost somewhere along the way.

So I sent it to three of my favorite theologians—guys I knew personally who had a strong and stellar grasp of theology. All three were married men with extremely busy ministry schedules. I thought I would just put it out there and see if any of them would bite, because I really wanted to know what they thought of Danylak's work. Was it for more than just singles? Was this for the whole church?

To my surprise and delight, all three responded almost immediately. Dr. Steve Brown was first, weighing in from a pastors' conference at 5:30 a.m. his time with two pages about his own journey as a pastor trying to help the singles in his church. He found Danylak's work to be a breath of fresh air on the topic and needed today in the church. Dr. Brown later interviewed Danylak on his radio program and again for his monthly *Pastors' Chat,* which goes out to more than five thousand pastors through the pastors' forum of Key Life.

Dr. Scott Horrell wrote at 2:00 a.m. his time, saying this work was very important and asking if I could connect him with the author so he could get permission to use the twenty-page synopsis for one of his seminary courses in Dallas. Since Danylak's book *Redeeming Singleness* was published, Dr. Horrell happily recommends it to his students.

World Team's own John Wilson wrote last, saying that he was impressed with Danylak's biblical theological approach. As a missiologist, John shared that the tribal people he worked with in Indonesia never really had singles, except for those who had been born handicapped. But he said reading this "makes me wish I could go back and teach them again about marriage and family, as there is a huge piece of Christology that got missed because I didn't address biblical singleness." John (now with the Lord) used Danylak's work to mentor missionaries in how to teach marriage, sexuality, and singleness.

A few months later all three men would write an editorial review for Danylak's book entitled *Redeeming Singleness: How the Storyline of Scripture Affirms the Single Life*. This book was published by Crossway, which also published John Piper's *This Momentary Marriage*. Both are highly recommended for their kingdom focus.

In the months that followed I remember putting out other little "nuggets" of these ideas with supporters and friends. In a retirement center in Denver, Colorado, I had lunch with a few widows and lifelong singles. I mentioned very briefly, in a couple sentences, how God had impressed some of these things on my heart. No one took the bait ... or so I thought.

The next day Shirley (eighty-three-years-young and never married) told me she had been thinking about what I had said all night. She looked me in the eye and said quite passionately, "Suzy, you're on to something here—you must keep pursuing it. This is so needed in our missions and churches and world today." She teared up and began to tell me story after story of times in her life when she had suffered because of people's lack of understanding of God's view on these things. Shirley is one of the gentlest, sweetest, most compassionate, least whiny Christians I've ever met. There is not a bitter bone in her body. But she had carried these wounds silently all these years, and that's why the truth hit her so hard. Her exhortation made me sit up and take notice. It felt almost prophetic.

Just weeks later, I was at a prayer meeting in British Columbia, Canada. The gathering consisted of several current and retired missionaries. They had asked me to share about church planting in France for forty-five to fifty minutes. So I shared for forty-five minutes on France and then added about five minutes to talk about the implications and concerns I had about our missions and churches thinking deeply about the biblical theology of both singleness and marriage. Again, I was brief.

Afterward, over lunch, a coworker, Gary, sat next to me and said, "Suzy, it was so good to hear how God is advancing his kingdom in Europe; and we've prayed with you for years, so this is encouraging. But I have to tell you, I really think that little part you shared at the end may be even more important to the worldwide church. This is huge! This matters in ways that extend far beyond Europe. Press on—I will be praying for you." Gary is married with two adult married children. His words were another confirmation and exhortation that I took from the Lord.

In a nutshell, a biblical theology of singleness gives us a broad understanding of marriage, sexuality, and singleness. We all understand how marriage points to the relationship of Christ and the church, but few understand how singleness points to kingdom realities too. Scripture has a high view of both marriage and singleness, but our churches rarely teach this. I am convinced that a deep understanding of this would help us better reach the lost with the message of the gospel, empower more singles and marrieds to use their marital status to point others to Jesus, and give us an attractive, compelling message about the body of Christ in the "Corinth-like" cultures where we minister. The New Testament mandate for all in the body of Christ—married, single, with or without children—is a call to make spiritual children and advance his kingdom. That's a high calling for each one of us.

In the years since, God has taken these ideas and opened unexpected doors. One of the people I shared the twenty-page document with was Dorcas Harbin from One Another Ministries (a member-care organization). She found it to be a valuable tool in working with mission groups in North Africa and Eastern Europe. Together, Dorcas and I organized a small gathering of single missionaries in 2009. Barry Danylak agreed to attend, and we met him for the first time there. He shared his work with us; and, as encouraging as it was, we realized that it could benefit many others.

In 2010, we gathered more missionaries, including married couples, with and without children. Married couples without children shared that they were deeply encouraged to see how the biblical theology spoke to them as childless couples. People in their situation had often felt misunderstood and hurt by well-meaning colleagues and churches. The assumption that married with children is the norm and preferred status for missionaries has left its wounds. Some of the singles said the theology "took the sting" out of their status. Couples with children saw implications for them and their families as well. All who attended were encouraged. From those events, Shoulder to Shoulder, a mission initiative sponsored by One Another Ministries, was birthed in 2011, and I became a member of the executive team. We believe solid biblical theology leads to sound practical theology.

Shoulder to Shoulder exists to come alongside cross-cultural workers, mission teams, organizations, and their leaders. We help them prepare for the realities and challenges of meaningful, effective cross-cultural life and ministry by encouraging ministry teams to value, integrate, benefit from, and empower every member. Our team offers training and workshops and a range of tools and resources for effectively equipping and empowering singles and marrieds working together in the Great Commission.

Later in 2011, I was able to introduce Barry Danylak to Dr. Larry Crabb. As Larry shook hands with Barry, he said, "So you're the author of *Redeeming Singleness!* You know, there have been many, many books, including a few of my own, written about Christian marriage. I think there are now over twenty-five thousand on the subject. But Piper was the first one to hit on the core essential that marriage is about glorifying God. And you, Barry, hit on that same thing about singleness. Thank you for reminding us of the most important part."

From 2012 to 2015, our Shoulder to Shoulder initiative hosted several gatherings and created a few tools and resources for missions. In 2016, it hosted a leadership summit in Spain. The response of the mission leaders was positive and promising. In attendance at that summit were Don and Sue Eenigenburg, with Christar. At the end of the event, Sue wondered aloud if the subject of married and single people working together on mission teams didn't merit a book. She later invited me to coauthor this book with her.

We hope this work will lend some practical help to our brothers and sisters in ministry around the world. We certainly pray it can contribute to healthy conversations in our mission organizations and on our ministry teams, for the sake of the Great Commission.

INTRODUCTION 2

An Invitation to More

It Started with an Invitation

THE INVITATION FROM SHOULDER TO SHOULDER, an initiative of One Another Ministries (see Appendix 1) came with specific information and goals for the summit.

I (Sue) had already been thinking about team relationships among single and married persons. In various training events, the leadership of Christar had been asking our single members what Christar had done well and what we had done poorly when it comes to caring for single missionaries. We were barely scratching the surface, but what we were hearing gave us pause. It made us want to do better, to make changes where we were weaker and continue to strengthen areas where we were doing well. Receiving the summit invitation added a sense of urgency.

At the summit, we learned a great deal about the biblical theology of singleness. I have heard many sermons on marriage and how God uses marriage to illustrate the image of Christ and his church, his bride. I don't remember ever hearing a message on singleness and how God uses single persons to reflect his glory and his all-sufficiency, as Danylak points out in Redeeming Singleness:

> Singleness lived to the glory of God and the furtherance of his kingdom testifies to the complete sufficiency of Christ for all things. The Christian is fully blessed in Christ, whether he or she is married or single, rich or poor, in comfort or duress. The distinctive calling of singleness within the church testifies to this truth.

> Paul distinguishes the spiritual gift or charisma of singleness by three elements. First, it is characterized by one who, by the grace of God, lives a continent life apart from marriage, that is, above reproach in the sexual arena. Second, it is distinguished as a life free from the distractions of a spouse and children, a life characterized by freedom and simplicity, which testifies to the complete sufficiency of Christ. Third, it is a life enabled for constant service to the King and the kingdom. It emulates the model of the eunuch who is ready and waiting to serve the King whenever and however he is called. (2010, 213)

Each of us, married or single, has a role to play in the kingdom of God. One is not elevated above the other. One is not more ideal than the other. Both have challenges and joys. Both have complete access to God the Father, through the Son, and can live by the power of the Holy Spirit however he leads us.

Because of these truths and because healthy team relationships are key to fruitful ministry across cultures, Suzy and I met to discuss working on this project together. I am blessed to be married, and I come into this with a married person's perspective. Suzy is blessed to be single, and she brings her perspective to this joint project. Together, we want to explore what the missions community can do to understand each other more, work together better, and as one body serve the Lord effectively under the headship of Christ.

It Continued with the Survey

In general, there are a lot more resources available for married couples than for single persons. Christena Cleveland (2018) points this out in one of her blog posts: "A quick search at Amazon.com reveals that for every 1 Christian book on singleness, there are 298 Christian books on marriage."

We began to research what had already been written about marrieds and singles working together on teams. We discovered that more had been written for married people in ministry than single people in ministry, although we have seen more about singleness in recent history. We also found that not much at all has been written about married and single people ministering together. It seems as if singles attend the seminars regarding singleness and married people do the same when workshops about marriage arise. This is good and helpful. However, there haven't been many training opportunities or materials written about married and single persons working together and how marital statuses may affect and influence relationships in ministry. This is only one factor in team relationships, of course, but it is a factor that is often overlooked.

Because of what we found—or rather didn't find—we contacted more than twenty-five organizations and asked if they would be willing to participate in our research about marital status, teams, and organizational life. Almost half responded affirmatively, and we sent them the survey to pass along to their members. Due to security measures, some individuals responded without specifying their organization. A copy of the letter and the survey are found in the appendix of this book.

The information we gathered from the survey has some limitations. We don't know how many copies were sent out, since we depended on mission agencies to send the survey to teams that met the requirements. So we don't know what percentage of the surveys that were sent out were completed and returned. However, we can still learn from the feedback that was received.

Several respondents did not like the numerical rating system of the survey. As a result, they sometimes answered with a zero even if the question applied to them, because they didn't like the other options. This might skew some of the data, as we ignored the zeros.

We encountered another difficulty with evaluating the answers in the comment section appropriately. For example, one question asked, "Does gender or marital status influence ministry opportunities in your organization? Please explain." Some responded, "No, but …" or "Yes, but …" So the answer seemed like a no or yes, but in reality the "but" added some information that clarified the meaning behind the respondent's answer.

Despite the limitations of the survey, the information gained has been invaluable in helping us know what organizations and teams are doing to help single and married people work together. We've also examined some weaknesses that were highlighted and what we as organizations and teams can do to improve. We've learned about the challenges and joys of team life from the married and single people who work together. In addition, we've discovered great ideas for building understanding, as well as learning what we can avoid that harms team relationships.

Who filled out the survey, and what are some of the things we learned?

And the Survey Says

If you aren't into numbers and percentages, this section might seem a bit dull! Taking the time to read it, however, will give you a foundation for understanding the survey results.

Let's start with the basics of who completed the survey. We received 289 responses to the survey, 200 of which were from women (69.2 percent). Slightly more married people responded: 159 married people (55 percent) filled out the survey, compared to 130 single people (45 percent). Of those who were single, only 15 were men. Here's a **breakdown of the ages:**

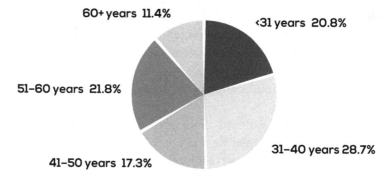

60+ years 11.4%

<31 years 20.8%

51-60 years 21.8%

31-40 years 28.7%

41-50 years 17.3%

As you can see, about half of the respondents were under 40 years old. Almost 40 percent were between 41–60. The rest were over 60. We are grateful for the span of ages that contributed to the survey.

To see the ministry experience represented, we also asked about the **number of years in cross-cultural service.**

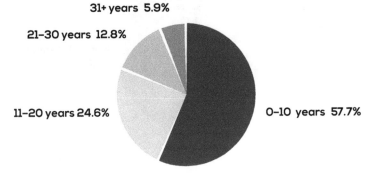

31+ years 5.9%
21–30 years 12.8%
11–20 years 24.6%
0–10 years 57.7%

Over half of those who completed the survey had been in ministry 10 years or less. About 37 percent had between 11–30 years of missionary experience. Those with more than 31 years of service numbered only about 6 percent.

At a recent Shoulder to Shoulder conference of single missionaries with ministry experience spanning 3–36 years, we noticed an increased awareness of generational differences, and the group was able to talk about some of them together. At times it was tense, but we came away with a better understanding of each other's generation. We now know more about some of the critical issues from each generation's perspective. Multigenerational teams must be intentional in seeking to understand and respect each other's views. Growing in awareness of these differences is essential.

Many roles were represented in the survey. Team leaders, church planters, medical personnel, educators, member care providers, and administrators, as well as many others, took the time to help in this research. We are deeply grateful. There was a wide range of **religious blocs among which missionaries were serving.**

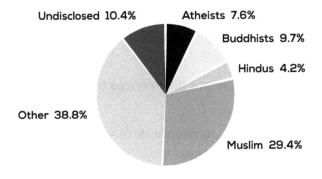

Undisclosed 10.4%
Atheists 7.6%
Buddhists 9.7%
Hindus 4.2%
Other 38.8%
Muslim 29.4%

The survey is weak from an international standpoint, since 76.8 percent of those who completed the survey were North American. **These other nationalities were included:**

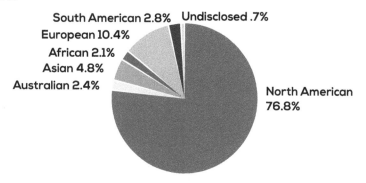

South American 2.8%   Undisclosed .7%
European 10.4%
African 2.1%
Asian 4.8%
Australian 2.4%

North American 76.8%

As a result, the survey is probably more valuable for North American sending agencies because the information reflects a majority of their members.

Regarding team makeup, it isn't surprising that 94 percent of respondents had experience with single women on their team, while only 6 percent had single men on their team. It is well known that there are many more single women serving across cultures than single men.

The survey contained thirty-seven statements that people could rate as "rarely," "sometimes," "often," or "almost always." The point of having just four choices was that there was no middle ground. Respondents were forced to choose between better or worse.

We were looking for significant differences in the data by comparing mean scores of different groups. How did the responses of married people notably vary from those of their single coworkers? Examining the data, we discovered marked discrepancies between married and single women as well. We also thought we should take into account major differences between men and women, as gender can often be a factor in team relationships as well. Three revelations emerged from the data:

- **There were sixteen significant differences based on marital status.**

- **There were six significant differences based on gender.**

- **There were thirteen significant differences between married and single women.**

There were eleven statements with which more married people than single people agreed:

1. My organization values single and married people equally.

2. The opinions of single and married women are equally valued.

3. Pre-field training in my organization intentionally prepares singles for missions.

4. I seek to meet the needs of others on my team.

5. The host culture I am in respects women regardless of their marital status.

6. There is good communication between married and single people on my team.

7. I have a way to process information after team meetings or from mission leadership.

8. Leadership in my organization requests my feedback on important issues.

9. Women are seen as sisters in Christ by the men on my team.

10. I am content in my current marital status.

11. I take time to listen to each member of my team.

There were five statements with which single people agreed much more than their married coworkers:

1. I thought team life would be like a family, but it does not provide the community I need.

2. I am seen as a little sister or little brother on my team who is not treated like an adult.

3. I do not get the help I need from others on my team due to my marital status.

4. More community ministry time is expected from single people than married people on our team.

5. I am seen as a perceived threat to the marriages of couples on my team.

The issues stemming from these sixteen differences form the basis for the remaining chapters of this book. But before moving to those chapters, we'd like to point out other significant differences that will also be addressed.

In addition to differences between married and single missionaries, *we found six significant discrepancies based on gender. Women agreed with the following statements more strongly than men:*

1. Single men tend to be more alienated from team life than single women.

2. I'm seen as a perceived threat to the marriages of the couples on my team.

3. I am seen as a little sister or little brother on my team who is not treated like an adult.

There were three statements with which men agreed more strongly than women:

1. Women are seen as sisters in Christ by the men on my team.

2. I am content in my current marital status.

3. I am encouraged to use my spiritual gifts and feel fully utilized in ministry.

You will notice there is a lot of overlap between these differences and those based on marital status. However, there are three issues with significant implications.

First, single men tend to be more alienated from team life than single women. It is surprising that women thought this was truer than men as a whole, but 40 percent of single men agreed with this statement. The married men didn't think this was a problem. However, it appears to be an issue, and we will address this in a later chapter.

Second, women didn't feel as encouraged to use their spiritual gifts and didn't feel as fully utilized in ministry as men did. We found this disturbing, as women, and we are thankful we can take a deeper look at this later in the book.

Third, men had a higher opinion than women about how they are treating the ladies on their teams as sisters in Christ. What does treating women as sisters in Christ look like? When Paul wrote to Timothy to treat "older women as mothers, and younger women as sisters, with absolute purity" (1 Tim 5:1–2), what did he have in mind? How do the challenges differ if the woman is married or single? How does culture play a role in the way men treat women? How do men and women have a healthy "sacred sibling" relationship in oversexed cultures while seeking to maintain moral purity? We think this topic deserves much discussion throughout our organizations and on our teams.

We also wanted to compare married and single women's responses to see if there would be any significant discrepancies. There were thirteen significantly different responses between married and single women; and, again, there was some overlap with the previous data about married and single people in general.

There were ten statements with which married women agreed significantly more than single women:

1. My organization values single and married people equally.

2. Pre-field training in my organization intentionally prepares singles for missions.

3. Pre-field training in my organization intentionally prepares married and single people to work together on teams in missions.

4. The opinions of single and married women are equally valued.

5. I seek to meet the needs of others on my team.

6. The host culture I am in respects women regardless of their marital status.

7. There is good communication between married and single people.

8. I have a way to process information after team meetings or from mission leadership.

9. I am content in my current marital status.

10. I take time to listen to each member of my team.

There were three statements with which single women agreed significantly more than their married sisters:

1. I thought my team would be like a family, but it does not provide the community I need.

2. I am seen as a little sister or little brother on my team who is not treated like an adult.

3. I do not get the help I need from others on my team due to my marital status.

There was a statistically significant difference of means comparing the total score of marrieds to the total score for singles, with a p-value, or probability value, of .036. (There is a brief explanation of p-value at the end of this chapter.) So married women overall more frequently approved the statements as true than single women. Though not all responses were significantly different, married women's agreement with the statements were almost always higher than that of their single sisters.

When there is a 96 percent chance that the married women's more positive responses were not random, what could be some of the reasons for this major difference? What are agencies doing or not doing that would make married women think more positively about these areas? How does team life influence their perspectives? What about the women themselves and their perceptions?

We've already noticed that more married than single people think that their organization values single and married people equally. Why might that be? One possible explanation is that married people, normally, are the majority within our organizations and in leadership. The majority usually assumes that if their needs are being met, everyone's needs are also being met.

Suzy has an interesting story and some questions to consider as she illustrates how easy it is for the majority to almost always be insensitive:

> I've spent most of my life in a marriage-majority mission. I think singles represent around 5 percent of our organization. I've noticed a tendency to gear everything to the "married with children" audience. That certainly makes sense when you can touch 90–95 percent of your mission that way. None of the insensitivity is intentional. It just happens. This is not just a married versus singles issue. In fact, cross-cultural teams with one dominant culture are generally insensitive too. The majority crowd always does what feels best and is easiest for them.
>
> I was stunned when I visited a team in another part of Europe. The team makeup was the exact opposite of my team in France. It was dominated by experienced singles in ministry, and the singles had been there the longest.
>
> I think there were nine of them, and they were welcoming a new couple to the team. As I sat in an Irish pub watching the group interact around a roaring fireplace, the young couple chased their eighteen-month-old around the pub. I was surprised to see how insensitive the singles were being to this couple. The couple had a great attitude, wanted to do everything to fit in with this team, and didn't want to call attention to their needs. Surprisingly, reversing the demographics did not solve the problem.
> It just showed me the effort a "majority" group must make to make minorities comfortable.
>
> Why are sensitive majorities so rare? Have you ever seen a majority group, culture, or race that was
> deeply sensitive to others in the minority? Surely the church should be the place where this is practiced and lived out.

When those in the minority bring up issues that need to be addressed, the majority is often surprised. Sometimes these concerns are summarily dismissed, as they are not felt by the majority. If a woman brings up an issue assertively, it is sometimes not heard—even if her concern is legitimate—because the messenger is seen as overbearing. When a man has a strong personality, sometimes (not always) he is seen as a leader. But when a woman has a strong personality, sometimes (not always) she is seen as aggressive.

In this book, we'd like to look at the most significant differences and talk about them through the lens of what we discovered through research. We also share from our own experiences as a single missionary and as a married missionary. Our goal is to look at the issues from both married and single perspectives and see what we can do to make our organizations better and our relationships stronger.

There are weaknesses that need to be addressed. Now that we know what some of them are, we can gather ideas and suggestions for improvement. There are strengths we can thank God for and upon which we can continue to build. Remembering, though, that our overarching purpose is more effective ministry and more fruitful relationships, we will take a look more intentionally at the weaknesses within our organizations and teams with the aim of developing good ideas and helpful tools.

A Brief Explanation of Significant Differences

Before examining the significant differences, what is it that determines whether a difference is significant? Rosanna Hess, the wonderful researcher who helped with the analysis of the data, explained the "p-value" to me (Sue). It is this number that determines whether a difference in results is significant. I understood it as she explained it, but I am still unable to communicate it to others! So, for a simple explanation, I went to Google and found a clear summary of p-value at http://www.dummies.com/education/math/statistics/what-a-p-value-tells-you-about-statistical-data/:

> A small p-value (typically ≤ 0.05) indicates strong evidence against the null hypothesis [the claim that is on trial], so you reject the null hypothesis.
>
> A large p-value (> 0.05) indicates weak evidence against the null hypothesis, so you fail to reject the null hypothesis.
>
> p-values very close to the cutoff (0.05) are considered to be marginal (could go either way). Always report the p-value so your readers can draw their own conclusions.

So if the *p*-value is .05, this means there is only a 5 percent chance that it is a random occurrence! Most likely, all p-values lower than .05 indicate significant differences.

Using the *p*-value of .05 as a cutoff, the following chapters reveal the statements about which there were statistical differences between married and single people's viewpoints.

Marrieds and Singles

(Suzy) Upon returning from a candidate assessment week with applicants to the mission, one leader was asked how it went. He responded, "Well, I guess it was OK, but we were disappointed that we only had single women applicants." That remark would be completely understandable *if* we had a high view of both singleness and marriage, as that would mean we risk not having enough couples and balanced teams. Sadly, at previous assessments, where there were only couples, there was no stated disappointment. The truth is that we need both. This remark suggested to me that the mission preferred married couples over singles and didn't have a high view of both marriage and singleness.

Sometimes I (Sue) am fearful when discussing issues revolving around marital status that some might think this book is intended to be one huge complaint against agencies and mission personnel for their lack of care for single cross-cultural workers. This is not true. Married and single relationship challenges can be an emotionally charged topic with a lot of historical context. Past hurts and other grievances may color one's perspective of what another person is saying. I have heard a single woman communicating an issue, and possibly she has mentioned it or similar issues before, and leaders dismiss the issue due to their perception of the person presenting it. Other times, a single person hears back from leadership but listens from the perspective of a person who didn't feel heard the first time, and as a result doesn't really give the leader a chance to explain fully where he or she is coming from.

Suzy and I desire to present what we've learned from the surveys in an unbiased way. Certainly our experiences have influenced our viewpoints, but as we've come together to discuss what we've learned we hope to communicate in a way that neutralizes past blame, minimizes bias, and maximizes good ideas and helpful tools for future fruitfulness.

We've all made mistakes; everyone miscommunicates. If there is one thing we've learned in ministry, it is that grace is needed in all our relationships. Single people must show grace to married people, and married people must show grace to those who are single. One of the saddest things that can occur in ministry is a lack of forgiveness in relationships that results in a root of bitterness. This damages our witness for Christ and must be addressed and changed by the Spirit of God.

It is our goal to share where agencies are—where we are strong, where we are weak, and how to improve for the benefit of all.

We pray that this research begins a fruitful dialogue between leadership and members—those who are married and single, as well as men and women. May we move forward in effective communication and healthy relationships. By God's grace, may we show each other grace as we look at the issues and strategize how to deal with them for his glory.

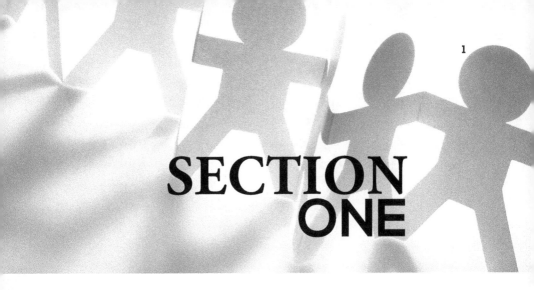

SECTION ONE

Issues Revealed from a Married's Perspective

As we examined the statements from the survey, there were eleven statements with which more married people than single people agreed. In this section, we look at areas in which significantly more married people thought certain statements were true than their single coworkers. The themes of the statements have been organized into five parts:

value (chapters 1–3),

training (chapter 4),

communication (chapters 5–7),

relationships (chapters 8–10), and

contentment (chapter 11)

CHAPTER 1

Equally Valuing =Valuing Equally

STATEMENT	MEAN
My organization values single and married people equally.	Married 3.58 Single 3.20 *P*-VALUE .000

More married people than single people thought that marital status had no bearing on the value organizations placed on single and married people. Single people are more likely to believe there is a difference in value. Reading through feedback in the survey, we concluded that single people felt less valued than those who are married.

Jeannie Lockerbie Stephenson points out that she had never heard the term "single missionary" until she became one:

> I had never run into the term "single missionary" until I became one. In the business and professional world a person is an executive, a teacher, or a nurse, not a "single" executive, teacher, or nurse. I was introduced to the term in missionary candidate seminar the year I joined ABWE. (2008, 1)

For some reason, we have felt the need, in the mission world, to distinguish between married and single missionaries. I (Sue) am not sure why, but it might prescribe or describe some of the issues we face!

As a married missionary woman, I had my own set of challenges. Years ago, when Don and I were visiting our organization's US office, we met with the staff for their time of prayer. We had four young children at the time and it was a delight to stop back in to see people who prayed for us and did so much for us in the States while we were overseas. Someone asked my husband to share about ministry. After he shared, it felt to me like someone finally realized I was also in the room and asked me to share as well. I don't remember why, but I sensed I was an afterthought. I am sure it was unintended. Possibly I was still suffering from jet lag. Maybe I was feeling insecure, fearful my ministry was less important than Don's and therefore projecting that onto others. Regardless of why, I felt slighted and therefore shared only a brief portion of what

I had prepared to share with supporters. I did not feel as valued as my husband, nor did I sense that my role and ministry were as valid to them as my husband's.

Afterward, one of the leaders suggested that I should be more prepared, because when we would go to churches I would probably be given opportunities to share about ministry. I was prepared. I had more to say. But I didn't because I didn't sense people really wanted to hear about me.

I didn't know how to put into words how I was feeling or why. It might have been my fault; it could have been theirs. The important point is that I didn't even talk about what I was feeling with those in the US office. So now, thirty-one years later, I still don't know if it was me or them or both! If I had it to do over again, my more mature self would say, "I don't know if it was me or my jet lag making me feel this way, but I felt less valued than my husband. Can we talk about it?" That would have helped me. It would have helped them. They might have gained a clearer understanding of how to communicate value to married missionary women. I might have gained encouragement, through that conversation, that I and my ministry were valued.

I thought single people would have an advantage in situations like this. When a single woman comes to the mission office or goes back for debriefing, she is asked directly about her ministry. No one asks her just to share about her family. No one discounts her if she is "only" homeschooling or mothering small children, while barely maintaining her sanity. She is seen as a professional full-time missionary. I imagined she would be valued and her ministry seen as a clear asset because it isn't mixed with ministry to a family in her home. Her opinion would be respected more because of her role in ministry. I thought she would be seen more as an equal in ministry than a married woman would be. Her opinion would be sought after because her role, on a day-to-day basis, isn't as divided as a married woman's; and her status would be seen as an asset.

According to the survey, I was wrong in my assumption that singles would feel more highly valued. Is it possible that organizations are somehow miscommunicating the value they think they are communicating to singles?

I (Suzy) would say I agree with Sue's assessment that when I'm interviewed at the home office, I'm respected as an adult with a vibrant ministry. I'm treated with fairness and asked to share my story and ministry with the support staff.

However, I sometimes feel more vulnerable in decisions or questions related to human resources. I remember, years ago, feeling called on the carpet about the length of my home assignment in a private interview with the personnel director. I had taken only five months as I needed to get back to the field. But I was questioned as though I'd taken too much time and was being extravagant. He even added that I should have included some educational training in the package. I was stunned, since several of my supporters had expressed concern that I had no opportunity for real rest.

I felt blindsided by the criticism I picked up from the director. As we waded through the itinerary of my home assignment and I explained my reasoning, he got out the policy manual. After looking at the numbers, he slowly retracted his criticism and said I could have taken several months more. It felt like he assumed I was cheating the mission or something.

There have been other occasions when it's been difficult to help with aging parents. My mission board was firm, stating that I could only have up to two weeks a year for family leave. I remember thinking, "Great—that would be for a funeral." Yet my married friends regularly took far longer periods visiting parents, children, and grandchildren, because one of them could "cover" for the other. I'm not against my married colleagues having freedom to deal with family issues, but it sometimes feels like singles don't have as much, if any, freedom in this area.

I've sometimes wished there was a man to defend me when someone assumes the worst or questions my integrity. I can't imagine leaders being so quick to assume the worst or asking the same probing questions of my married counterparts.

These are two of our stories. When asked on the survey how their organizational leadership viewed singles, respondents gave a wide variety of responses. Comments that reflected valuing singles included:

> "[I feel] like a valuable contributor to the work of the kingdom of God. I feel no different value, treatment, or expectations on me simply because I am a single lady."

> "I believe that singles are valued in our organization. From my perspective, I have seen ways in which singles have unique struggles which require additional (or maybe just different) support, interaction, and energy. Even so, I have never seen that influence the value the leadership places on singles."

> "As a VP, I mentor two people each year. Both of my mentees this year are single women who have great leadership potential."

> "[Singles are viewed] as incredibly valuable in their ability to give themselves to work in hard places without the burden of family that married couples have to carry."

> "[Singles are viewed] as persons with an equal status and standing. Singles are paid less, however, than couples. There are other financial inequalities that are too complex to explain here."

"I believe our organization is growing in caring for and empowering singles on the field, especially women. It is a slow process, but there is movement."

"I have always had the impression that the leadership has a very high view of singles in our organization. A number of singles have roles in leadership, and I have always felt that a high priority is placed on making sure singles receive care and that the needs of singles are always discussed in training. Special events and discussions are always available for singles at conferences and retreats."

"I have been approached by leadership and asked how I feel about it. This leader encouraged me by pointing me to some resources, and he made me feel appreciated. I have never felt like I don't have room to share my thoughts about things, and I have never felt discriminated against."

"It seems to me that [singles] are viewed as people who are treated and evaluated with the same criteria as married people. If they have talent, skills, diligence, etc., in particular areas, they will be given appropriate responsibility, authority, and influence."

"I feel that my marriage gives me resources that my single colleagues lack. On the other hand, I believe that their singleness gives them a freedom in ministry and work that I lack. So we have something to offer each other."

There were also some comments that expressed concerns about how singles were viewed by the leadership in their organization:

"If single women are assertive, I think they are sometimes viewed as malcontents or aggressive. [Leaders] often feel more protective of young single women than single men or families. [Singles] are seen as capable, called, and effective."

"They view singles well and aren't afraid to use them in ministry. However, I feel our voices aren't heard as much as others.'"

"I think we are valued for the jobs we can and do do. Because we don't have 'families' on the field, we are tasked with more responsibility. Comments are made [about]how easy we have it, and the 'If you only knew the challenges of marriage, you wouldn't sign up' sayings just about destroy any could-be relationships."

"I am not aware of a particular 'view' of singles. I do know that, in evangelical circles, matrimony is seen as ideal and singlehood as less than ideal."

"[Leaders] are mostly great. The only issues come when they expect singles to maybe work conferences or other times so that families can be together. Very annoying. Also annoying when married colleagues get away with using 'family' as [an] excuse for laziness!"

"Most often [we're viewed] as valuable people. But I have sometimes seen rules in place that imply a single woman is a temptation for men, while not taking into account that things happen between married people as well. So [there is] a kind of false dichotomy that singles are more tempted or tempting than married people."

"Currently we have one single guy on the team. We will have a girl joining us soon. Our team leader has mentioned possibly finding another male single who could come on, but dissuaded another girl because he states that two single girls on a team can sometimes cause team dysfunction."

"I think they give lip service to valuing equally, but I think married people get more 'benefit of the doubt.' A married pastor/church planter is going to have higher automatic regard from others than a single. A single person in the same role is going to have to prove themself more."

"There are many of us, so I think they value us. In a lot of ways, we are more flexible because we don't have to think about families and have more time to commit to relationships among our host culture. I have noticed, however, at conferences put together by our organization that there are tons of support for families, with tons of workshops and resources for marriages/third-culture kids/homeschooling on the mission field. I think maybe there could be more single support."

"[We are viewed] as important parts of missions. My specific team leadership I think has been wonderful. However, for higher leadership (big decisions and meetings) only men are involved, so it does concern me that singles (particularly single women) may not have a voice at that level."

"Singles are valued, but at the end of the day families are always given more priority."

"On the one hand, our organization would praise singles and say how useful they are. On another, they tend to be placed on the bottom of the power structure, and their voices are not always heard. When trouble comes, they are sometimes treated as the most dispensable parts of the team. I have been aware of several abusive team relationships, where single ladies were basically told to shut up and submit, or else go. Those in leadership seemed to be very unaware of the signs of abuse. When the ladies spoke about their problems, their loyalty and obedience was put into question, and they were accused of being rebellious. I have heard some leaders speak of single ladies as being a major responsibility and a potential liability to a team. This is so demoralizing and just not true. Single ladies need encouragement and support, yes, but not parenting, not a bunch of monitoring; and they don't need someone else to make all their decisions."

An interesting insight is that the comments were hardly ever all positive or all negative; rather, they were mixed. So organizations are showing value in some ways, are progressing in other ways, and need to intentionally make some changes, as well, in how they are attempting to show value to their members. One comment that resonated with me was, "Unless the team leader values both singles and marrieds equally, no change is ever going to be [implemented] and the 'single' life will always be seen as less." How important it is to value our brothers and sisters and to communicate that value to them!

One possible reason behind not communicating value to our single coworkers could be that the church and many mission leaders are unaware that they automatically equate marital status with maturity. Singles sometimes feel as if they aren't considered mature or capable because they are not married. If someone isn't seen as capable, they are going to feel less valued.

Christena Cleveland (2018) gives some suggestions for how to embrace the singles in our lives:

- **AFFIRM THAT MARITAL STATUS ISN'T CORRELATED WITH GODLINESS OR MATURITY.** Many single people feel that they are often automatically stereotyped as spiritually immature, morally dangerous, and unsuitable for leadership *simply because they're single*... .

- **CELEBRATE SINGLE PEOPLE.** If you get married and/or have a baby, Christians will pull out all the stops to celebrate you. That's a good thing! But Christians should also recognize that many single adults never get celebrated with such fanfare. We might not be walking down the aisle or gestating a baby, but God is doing some amazing things in our lives—from the "monumental" (such as helping us obtain degrees, launch ministries/businesses, pay off college loans) to the "mundane" (such as helping us serve our neighborhoods, pray for each other).

As mission agencies affirm the single marital status and celebrate singles in their organizations, they communicate value to these people and their status. Cleveland (ibid.) also lists ways that those who are married can embrace singles. Though written for the church, her ideas can be relevant to mission agencies as well.

When married people recognize their privilege, they can work to restore balance by:

- Listening well

- Being an advocate and raising questions (e.g., How can we make our "family camp" relevant and inclusive for singles?)

- Inviting single people to the table (hiring, boards, preaching, conference speakers, etc.)

- Making sure that issues that are pertinent to singles are raised in meetings, from the pulpit, while vision casting, at retreats, at conferences, etc.

- Reframing policy, values, and expectations so that married people are no longer the gold standard.

We've already mentioned listening well, but as advocates for our single members, what questions do we need to be asking? Do we know what issues are pertinent to them? How do our policies reflect value to our single members?

One respondent wrote about the need for an advocate:

Conflicts will happen and need to be addressed.
However, a single may have no advocate or someone to turn to if
there is a conflict. Who do they go to if they're having a problem
with another teammate or the team leader or team leader's
wife? Is there a safe and a trusted person to go to?

Some of the respondents expressed concerns regarding policy from organizational leadership. How is the support determined for a single missionary as opposed to a married couple? What does going to a conference look like for a single person who doesn't feel comfortable sharing a room?

At an organization's recent training conference, one single woman thanked the organizers for asking her for her rooming preference—Would she like a roommate or not? She said she had never been asked that before at a conference! To show value to her, they covered her preference for a single room financially. This might not always be possible, as organizational finances can be tight. Sometimes the person can pay the cost difference. But asking their preference honors them. To not be given an option or to consistently be penalized for a preference can be devaluing.

How does a single person's vacation time compare to a married person's? When there is a family emergency, is there a difference between how organizations handle time off for those who are married and those who are single? One single missionary woman commented on the survey:

Our leadership is much less forgiving of singles when it comes
to requesting time off. Married people and leadership (who are
married) spontaneously take off for "family time" without trouble.
But any of the singles who request time off are looked down on
and even get called in to explain themselves.

Seeing these differing responses to requested time off sends a devaluing message to those who are single.

We appreciate that the vice president of an organization is mentoring two single women. He saw their leadership potential and is taking action. I am positive that these two women feel valued. Their potential was observed, and the leadership is initiating the development of that potential.

One of the significant differences between the responses of men and women was that more men than women felt that they were encouraged to use their gifts and felt fully utilized. Of course, women are responsible to develop and use their spiritual gifts whatever their circumstances. Encouragement does help, though.

STATEMENT	MEAN
I am encouraged to use my spiritual gifts and feel fully utilized in ministry.	Married 3.02 Single 3.31 P-VALUE .011

Whether intentional or not, the message of this discrepancy seems to indicate a lack of value of female coworkers and their ministries. This could be evidenced by failing to provide training opportunities for women. In the distant past it was common—due to limited finances and having predominantly male leadership—for our agency, and possibly others, to invite mostly men to leadership or strategic-planning meetings.

For the married woman with young children, ministry outside of the home is limited. When my four children were younger, my travel was limited due to their education, and my energy was limited due to ministry in my home and community. I didn't have a lot of extra time or energy for attending many conferences. I appreciated when I was given opportunities to learn. However, it was a bit sad to me that I was unable to go to events when men were free to do so. I am especially grateful that as my children grew older and I had more time to invest in training opportunities, that those opportunities were available. Being asked to speak at some of these events was a delight.

I don't remember leadership ever saying no to initiatives that I presented, and I felt that my voice was heard. Some wives/mothers have been able to come to training events or conferences, and their husbands have stayed home to care for the children. Families can work this out. Both could be invited. Providing childcare is vital when we want mothers to attend conferences. Some missions invite the person with the right skills and gift sets for the training opportunity and make invitations based on strengths to be developed, not gender.

When organizations see women gifted as trainers, it is vital that they use them! When women are gifted in leadership, find ways that they can use their strengths. Whatever your view on women in leadership, how can women use their God-given spiritual gifts? Some women who aren't being utilized by their organizations resign. However, even when they stay, their gifts are often more welcomed by other agencies, or they bless field personnel where they live and where they can use their strengths.

Today we see mission leadership being much more proactive in inviting women to training events. Opportunities to influence and lead are more available for women in organizations. Organizations are also becoming more intentional about inviting younger workers, international partners, and other different voices than those they invited in the past.

Encouraging women to use their gifts, providing arenas for them to use their strengths, and effectively utilizing over half of our workforce is for the greater good of the kingdom.

In his article "It's Not My Daughter's Job to Teach Me About Women," Esau McCaulley shares his journey in growing to value his sisters in Christ:

> More than anyone else, Christian women have played a discipling role in this process. I'm speaking in particular of the slow work of grace that comes from listening to them and then reading the Scriptures afresh with their wisdom in mind. Some of what I've learned I know from a distance through the ministries and scholarship of these women, but others are personal friends of mine. All of them have helped deepen my understanding of what it means to love my sisters as God loves them: to stand up against sexist attitudes in male-dominated groups; to respect the competence of the women around me; to honor proper boundaries while also treating them as friends and colleagues, not as dangers or temptations; and to recognize their gifts and advocate for the exercise of those gifts in the church and, in my case, the academy. (2018)

Good Ideas and Helpful Tools

From Survey Respondents:

"THROUGH DISCUSSIONS WITH THE TEAM on roles and expectations of each team member, we talked about the unique situations of each single and married member of the team; i.e., rather than just lump singles into one category, we looked at who they are and what their gifting was and set roles and expectations accordingly. We did the same with married members (with and without children)."

"I'VE BEEN BOTH SINGLE AND MARRIED on the same team (was single, left the team for three years to get married and have kids, then returned with husband/kids to the same team and field). From that perspective I think that both are hard and have their own challenges. In both situations I was put into a box in some way or another, but I've loved both situations and the relationships I have from both. Knowing how it felt to be the single, I try to put into our lives and practices those things I would have appreciated as a single: inviting singles on holidays/weekends/trips/meals, asking if they want to babysit but not expecting, talking with them about ministry and not just my home, making sure if I hear something from my husband that they too get information relevant to them, asking them what they need/want from me, asking them if there are practical things my husband or I can help with. (I hated having to do everything as a single.)"

"I HAVE LEARNED A LOT about what it means to be a single female on the mission field during my time with the mission. I think I am valued and respected, and that has nothing to do with my marital status. We had a meeting with all of the ladies on our team (which is quite large, about twenty) and we discussed the issue of singleness versus marriage on our team. It was a very good meeting. We shared our thoughts about the other side and we listened to the hardships and struggles that we face. We left feeling more loved and encouraged than when we came. The main thing I got out of it was that I can feel free to spend time with the families even if they don't invite me over."

"I REALLY VALUE THE INVESTMENT that the single women on our team have made in my kids. They love on my kids and enjoy them. They take time to get to know them and give them godly advice. They fill in some of the 'family' we left behind. I also love being able to be friends with the single women on my team. Since they aren't tied up with family obligations, I don't feel like I'm taking away from their family time when I hang out with them!"

"MY HOST CULTURE SAYS that singleness is a negative thing (particularly for young women) and means you are less important and less worthy. It also says that sex is owed by the woman to the man in exchange for the privilege of being in a dating relationship. However, the singles on my team are able to show that we are different and find our identities in Christ, not in our marital status or having sex. So in that way, the singles are especially valuable in ministry, particularly to younger people."

Application Questions

- What conversations need to happen and what practices need to change to show value to coworkers?
- What would it look like to receive feedback successfully?

CHAPTER 2

Your Opinion Matters

STATEMENT	MEAN
The opinions of single and married women are equally valued.	Married 3.50 Single 3.25 *P*-VALUE .010

Valuing coworkers also means valuing their opinions. More married people thought that marital status had no effect on the value of women's opinions. Single people saw disparity.

One single woman responded in the survey how she felt in comparison to married women: "Single women are often not taken as seriously as a married woman. My training and ministry experience were sometimes discounted." Another single woman wrote, "Married people can be condescending toward singles (assuming those who aren't married are less mature). Singles can be overly sensitive toward the slightest hint of that condescension."

A married woman wrote, "It has been my experience that our organization values the opinions of single women above those of married women. They are asked to participate in leadership and invited to vision conferences held by our organization, while the marrieds are not."

There are differing views and varying experiences for single and married women. As a married woman, one of the things that makes me (Sue) feel that my opinion matters is to be asked for it—not necessarily as part of a group, though that is great too. But if someone asks me individually about a matter about which I am knowledgeable, I feel as if my voice matters. If someone asks me to be on a task force in an area in which I have skills that would help, I sense that I am a valued member of our organization.

One single responded in the survey that she has seen progress in her organization but is uncertain if gender, rather than marital status, was the reason she felt unheard:

> I think leadership is beginning to recognize the value of singles, especially on our field. It was not always this way. There were many times that I felt like I wasn't being listened to. When I look back, I wonder if that was just because I was a woman and it had nothing to do with my marital status.

Leadership must be intentional in seeking feedback and valuing the opinions of over half of their membership. Traditionally, most mission leaders have been men. If leaders are discussing strategic initiatives or planning future ministry opportunities, they may meet or send emails to each other to get feedback on proposals. Without meaning to, they may be missing the perspectives of female coworkers who could add significant insights to the conversation and ultimately to the direction in which to move forward. Women also cannot assume that they are not asked to be on task forces or to take on leadership roles because of their gender or marital status. It could be an issue of capability or gifting.

I have really appreciated our international director looking for people to serve on his council based not on marital status or gender but on skill sets and gifting. He looks at what he needs; he looks at objectives and who could help move the mission forward in church planting among least-reached peoples.

No one wants to sit on a council or be on a committee as a "token" person. No one in their right mind would want me on a committee discussing financial audits or technological advances for kingdom purposes. I am all about the kingdom, but I have little to give when topics are outside of my expertise. However, if there is a need for someone to talk about team dynamics or communication, I could be an asset.

In my role as director of women's ministry, it is fine to ask me for my opinion on issues pertaining to women in cross-cultural ministry. I understand that this can be helpful when trying to understand some things from a woman's point of view, and I am delighted to share common struggles or how women in our organization might feel about a certain issue. But also ask me about other things as a mission member! What do I think about the vision statement? How can we encourage our teams to live out the body of Christ and family of God to be a more effective witness to unbelieving communities? In what new areas could we proclaim the gospel in communities where few have heard it? I love brainstorming and purposeful interaction.

Many women in our organizations are untapped resources. Women who have had successful careers and have been called by God to missions sometimes feel as if they have been demoted when their expertise is discounted because of gender.

"I feel like the men's opinions matter much more than the women's.... All the ministry leaders are men. And so, as a single woman, it feels like I have a double disadvantage."

"I know of single women who were passed over for jobs that married men who were less qualified took. I know of a number of single, well-qualified women who left the organization because their skills were not being used to their potential."

Comments like these suggest that the lack of value being shown is a gender issue and not a marital one.

Men did not see this as an issue. Over 90 percent of single men and 70 percent of married men thought the marital status of women had no effect on the value of women's opinions. We may need to ask what valuing someone's opinion means. While men may say that they value what women have to say, they may not think to ask women for their opinion. They continue in their set patterns of gleaning information from each other—although if a woman was in the room and spoke up, they would probably value her contribution. In some cases, it may be that men don't think too little of women; they just don't think often enough to ask for a woman's opinion.

Marital status is an issue to women, however, as we see the discrepancy in sensing value is highlighted between single and married women.

STATEMENT	MEAN
The opinions of single and married women are equally valued.	Married 3.48 Single 3.23 *P*-VALUE .037

I was surprised that single women don't feel their opinions are as valued as married women's opinions. I always thought that single women were seen more as strategic partners, with less distractions on the home front. Seasons of life affect ministry, especially for missionary mothers. I remember being unable to talk as authoritatively on missional issues when I was mother with small children. Single women could and did! The team seemed to listen to and heed their comments. Single women were more likely to be on councils. I was involved, but more consumed with ministry in my home. I participated in meetings, but when strategies and mission opportunities were being discussed I felt like I took a back seat. Single sisters were in the thick of it.

Suzy remembers several team gatherings during which the women were in the kitchen discussing their kids and the men were in the living room talking strategy or mission issues. She was always torn about which group to join. She was interested in both, but in reality she identified more closely with the day-to-day activity of the men in ministry than of the women. Their season of life revolved around small children and school. Even though Suzy loved those kids dearly and their moms were her close friends, she often felt more drawn to the men's conversations.

There may be other reasons why single women don't feel their opinions are as valued as married women's. Maybe single women think that wives are represented, as their husbands hear their views. This is probably true, whether the husbands want to hear them or not! However, this may be reflective of the way in which single women perceive married women's influence on their teams and not an indicator that single women's opinions aren't valued. Maybe this would be more of a sense of influence than value if this is the case.

How can organizations show value to all of their members' opinions? This leads us to the next chapter about organizations requesting feedback from their members.

Good Ideas and Helpful Tools

From a Survey Respondent:

"I HAVE BEEN BOTH SINGLE AND MARRIED on my same team (though the makeup of the team has shifted greatly throughout the eleven years I have been here). I can say there are pros and cons to being married and single, but there are certainly things that all women can connect with each other on. I would encourage teams to have women's times and men's times, as well as all-team times, and just encourage people to cross barriers. There is a lot to be enjoyed about each other."

Our Recommendations:

- **ASK FOR OPINIONS.** Delve deeper by asking questions to gain background information and a greater understanding of others' reasoning.

- **THANK PEOPLE FOR SHARING** their opinions, whether you agree with them or not.

- **ACT ON GOOD SUGGESTIONS** and build on good ideas.

- **INTENTIONALLY INVOLVE ALL MEMBERS**—single and married men as well as single and married women—in discussing relevant mission challenges, strategy, and vision. These discussions should not be limited to only a few.

Application Question

- What is involved in showing value to opinions different from yours?

CHAPTER 3

Feedback Wanted ... or Is It?

STATEMENT	MEAN
Leadership in my organization requests my feedback on important issues.	Married 2.69 Single 2.46 P-VALUE .036

More married people thought their feedback on important issues was sought after than single people did.

If mostly men are in leadership roles and they are looking for feedback, it might be that the group email or Skype call only includes the male leaders who report to them. If some of those leaders are married, they might ask their spouses what they think. But if there aren't many single leaders, when is the feedback of singles requested? It would take an intentional extra step to ask single men and women, and sometimes in the busyness of life and ministry that intentional extra step is not taken. But we suggest it is needed.

Not utilizing the diverse voices within an organization limits its resources and the varied perspectives of its members who enable it to make better decisions. Leaders need to be even more intentional to request feedback from teams whose members come from a variety of cultural backgrounds and marital statuses. World Team now refers to these teams as "multi-situational teams."

How do mission agencies request feedback these days? They can use surveys, interviews, forms, and simple conversations. Survey Monkey (surveymonkey.com) seems to be a quick and easy way to gather feedback; Microsoft forms are also efficient. Making the surveys easy to complete and return is important. As organizations become more international, they may face additional challenges in obtaining input from those outside of the country in which the organization is based. More relational cultures and power distance leadership models would not respond well to direct questions or impersonal ways of responding. Even for people from a Western background, surveys sometimes detract from more relational ways of gathering feedback. When possible, face-to-face meetings or phone calls are better for getting information and developing relationships.

When leaders want to move forward, it is wise to ask for feedback. Sometimes they listen and move forward as planned, while other times they listen and change course. If input is never heeded, members may feel that their feedback is unnecessary and consequently lack the desire to continue to give it.

One leader shared how he was able to invite dialogue and put feedback into practice:

> There was an article on singleness in the Dallas Seminary magazine. I brought it to the office and showed it to one single lady. She passed it around and then came back to me on how we as a leadership team could be more encouraging. This was very positive and helpful. We should be looking to have this kind of exchange more often.

Other missionaries put it this way:

> "They are beginning to see us. Traditionally, I think also due to most of us [singles] being women, they sort of liked to keep us in our box. More recently they are beginning to ask more of us to attend feedback sessions about strategy and future leadership development."

> "It's really, really important that singles get to have the ear of those in authority, as well as wives, whether their husbands are in leadership or not."

Asking for and receiving feedback is essential for good leadership and making wise decisions. Listening to those who are affected by our decisions is wise. Receiving feedback on our training material makes our training better. We will look at training in our next chapter.

Good Ideas and Helpful Tools

In his book *If You Want to Walk on Water, You've Got to Get Out of the Boat,* John Ortberg (2001, 62) writes about Parker Palmer, who was offered a job. As he was trying to decide what to do, he used a Quaker tradition of gathering feedback to help him think it through. "The Quakers have a tradition where, when faced with an important decision about calling, they gather a half-dozen friends to serve as a 'clearness committee.' This committee gathers primarily to ask questions so as to discern God's calling more clearly.

Ortberg describes what this process is like:

> In the Quaker tradition, a clearness committee does not come together to give you advice. (Lots of people will do that without you asking.) And it certainly does not need people who have their own agenda for your life. The primary job of this group is simply to ask questions, listen thoughtfully, and then pray for a sense from God for his calling on your life.

I need people who will help me ask questions like:

- What do I enjoy doing for its own sake?

- What do I avoid doing? Why?

- For what do I wish to be remembered?

- How might the offer of money or promotion sidetrack me from my true calling?

- What would my life look like if it turned out well? (ibid., 68)

We would recommend using a clearness committee for some issues that need feedback. Another option is a "peer consultation process." During a leadership training event with Christar, Lowell Bliss, who is an experienced church planter and leader and the director of Eden Vigil, presented a peer consultation process in which a person comes to a small group to present a leadership challenge. The purpose is to get feedback and new perspectives from peers and to hear from unusual voices. The Kansas Leadership Center presents this method (adapted from the Cambridge Leadership Association) for gathering feedback in *For the Common Good: Participant Handbook* (O'Malley, McBride, and Nichols 2014, 61–62). With the authors' kind permission, we share the peer consultation guidelines.

Case Presentation

5 minutes

Goal for the Case Presenter

To present a leadership challenge.

- What is the adaptive challenge?
- Who are the major players? What are their conflicting perspectives and interests?
- What are your strengths with the major players?
- What action have you taken or are thinking about taking in reference to the challenge?
- What are your real stakes and interests?
- Are there any hidden issues?
- What have I learned about my adaptive challenge so far?

Data Gathering Questions

10 minutes

Goal for the group

To understand the adaptive challenge and the complexities surrounding it, and to gather information to help you conduct diagnostic brainstorming in the next phase.

- Who are the major players? What are their formal relationships? Informal alliances?
- Where is the senior authority on the issue?
- Who are the unusual voices in this situation, and have you sought them out?
- What has the presenter done so far to work on the problem? What has the presenter decided not to do?
- Why are you working on this?
- What do you care about related to this challenge?
- What would success look like to the presenter?

Diagnostic Brainstorming

15 minutes

*NOTE: Case Presenter does not speak!

Goal for the Group

To interpret what is happening, offer alternative interpretations and illuminate new ways to understand the case.

- What are the case presenter's stakes: risk of real or anticipated loss, sense of personal competence, pressure to maintain loyalties?

- What issues or values does the presenter represent in the case? Do you see/hear competing values?

- What are the underlying or hidden issues? What are the value choices each has to make?

- How does the situation look to the other players? What is the story they are telling themselves?

- What options are off the table for the presenter and why?

- What has the presenter contributed to the problem? What is her/his piece of the mess?

- What possible adaptive, conflictual or systematic interpretations has the presenter been understandably unwilling to consider?

- What is the level of disequilibrium in the system?

- What are the relevant factions in this challenge, and what do they care about, who are they loyal to and what are some of their potential losses?

- For real change to happen, who has to do the work on this? Who else?

- What would it look like for the presenter to "start where they are"?

- What would success look like to the players other than the presenter?

Action Step Brainstorming

5 minutes

*NOTE: Case Presenter does not speak!

Goal for the Group

To offer possible new initiatives, smart risks and experiments for the case presenter to try to move the challenge forward.

- What smart experiments could be undertaken? Which KLC leadership competency subpoints seem relevant?
  1. Does the presenter need to raise or lower the heat?
  2. How might the presenter need to "manage self" differently?
  3. What would it look like for the presenter to "start where they are"?
- What are low-risk tests of some of the ideas discussed?
- What courageous conversations need to take place?
- What new partnerships or relationship shifts need to happen?
- What could the presenter watch for or monitor as signs of progress on this adaptive challenge?

Presenter Reflections

5 minutes

Goal for the Case Presenter

Not to resolve the case!
This time is intended for the presenter to share initial reactions to the process and ask specific questions that he/she is now pondering.

- Comment on what has been heard. The idea is that the presenter will "rent" the ideas, trying them out rather than "buying" them or defending against them.
- Identify any action step(s) you may undertake in the next six weeks.

Group Debrief

5 minutes

Goal for the Group

To "get on the balcony" and reflect on how well
the consultation went and how to improve in the future.

- What did the group accomplish and what did it avoid?
- What default behaviors did participants observe?
- Did we make adaptive, conflictual and systemic interpretations?
- Did we identify the adaptive challenge?
- What could be done to improve consultations in the future?

Application Question

- What would it look like to receive feedback successfully?

CHAPTER 4

Effective Training Doesn't Come Easy

STATEMENT	MEAN
Pre-field training in my organization intentionally prepares singles for missions.	Married 2.98 Single 2.35 P-VALUE .000

It seems wise to have separate training for issues specific to marital status, but organizations must be more intentional in training us to work together well. It is great to have separate men's and women's sessions in trainings. The question that remains, though, is "How can we be more intentional in how we work together, as well as understand and help each other?" It seems that meeting together would provide more needed interaction and open doors to begin communicating about issues that affect each missionary.

A mission-training director once asked one of their organization's single missionaries, "How are we doing with singles?" Her response was, "Well, I don't think you do anything to hinder us, but I'm not sure you do anything to help us either."

It is possible that some agencies feel that not hindering is helping enough. Some mission agencies are implementing solid biblical training in the area of singleness for all missionaries. One training director responded about adding a biblical theology of singleness to their training, "That's a member-care issue, not a training issue." We maintain that it is a member-care issue because it isn't a training issue. Of course, it can be both; but one reason it develops into a more serious member-care issue is because it often isn't addressed in training.

Married people were more likely to think that pre-field training for singles was intentional and therefore probably adequate. Single people tended to say the training for them was not intentional, mainly because they felt it was weaker than those who are married think it is. This shows they desire more intentional training for singles before leaving for their field of service. Many of the principles taught in pre-field training are not all that different for married and single people.

We all need to learn about culture stress, language learning, conflict management, and time management. It could be that training weaknesses appear when we talk about applying what we learn and in the examples that are shared.

Suzy shares some insight about training for singles from her experience in a church plant, where she looks at marriage versus singleness preparation:

> I was sitting in a local church plant in Europe when a colleague came to share his ministry in premarital counseling with our church. André was passionate about the need for marriage preparedness for couples who were engaged. We were sympathetic to the need for this. However, I looked around our group and noticed there wasn't one engaged couple in the room. In fact, the audience included several married couples with children, and a few singles, never-married, like myself, divorcees and widows. No one was dating or engaged. Surely someday someone will need André's help. But it got me to thinking: Why don't we have a singleness preparedness course? Not everyone will marry, but everyone will be single at least for some portion of their life. Why don't we prepare people for godly singleness? At least that's a course that would apply to everyone!

What are we doing as mission agencies (and churches) to train people in godly singleness as well as in serving across cultures as a single person?

To see what some agencies are doing now in their training, read these comments from the survey:

> "Singles sat through all the sessions about kids and family, but [also] at a separate session with just singles. It would maybe be helpful for the couples to sit through that session as well or have a separate session on supporting singles."

> "I remember sitting in a session with a panel of married and singles … discussing the pros/cons/challenges/joys of a mixed team. It was extremely beneficial and should happen at every orientation."

> "[Training] prepared me for the host culture's view of single women and the way I need to behave so as not to offend, but it didn't prepare me for team life with married and single people working together."

"Nearly all of the training—conflict resolution, peacemaking, security, support development, etc.—was aimed toward married couples. Not that a single couldn't get anything out of it, but the practicality (examples, case studies, etc.) was all based around marriage and couples."

"Additional training would be helpful for those headed to the field when they are doing their cross-cultural training—because, in reality, singles and married are cross-cultural."

Respondents appreciated the efforts their organizations put into training singles, but some said it wasn't enough. There were those who said the training was general enough that it would be applicable to all. However, it seems that, overall, singles would appreciate more intentional, meaningful training than what is currently being offered.

Have we looked at the illustrations and case studies in our training materials? Are there illustrations where single people find themselves represented? Are there realistic scenarios with not just stereotypical versions of single people? Have you considered asking people from all aspects of your mission culture to look over materials before they are released or policies are put in place? Inviting feedback before things are done can prevent unnecessary heartache and angst.

Do we have many single leaders? Are single people involved in planning training events and training others? Are organizations affirming of singleness and proactively honoring singles' ministries through their training conferences?

One single woman shared that in a training module almost all of the examples used were of married people—except one. And that one seemed like it was thrown into the mix at the last minute and was far removed from what singles actually experience. The scenario seemed to be a married person's perception of what a single might face.

I remember reading through a case study in a training course for our whole mission. There was one example of a single person, and their issues were depression, loneliness, laziness, and boredom—pathetic, really. As I read this single's story I remember thinking, "I can't think of any single missionary I've ever known who is like this." If anything, they are workaholics with large networks of friends, and their life is anything but boring!

By being intentional to include both married and single people as trainers in our pre-field training, by addressing issues and opportunities faced by individuals of different marital statuses, and by encouraging dialogue between members in varying family situations, we can increase the effectiveness of our training. We must also remember this in other trainings as well, not just pre-field!

From the surveys, we can see that organizations offer training for single and for married people. From what we've gathered, there are usually separate sessions for married people and single people. Not many organizations put these groups together when talking about marriage and singleness. How can we build toward understanding what each other will be going through if we don't sit in those sessions together? This isn't to say that it is never beneficial for married and single people to receive separate training, but wouldn't it be more beneficial if the two groups met together?

Organizational trainers need to evaluate their current programs to see what is effective in preparing single and married missionaries, both for service in their fields and ministry alongside each other. How can we be more intentional in training in some of the issues that married and single people might face on a team? Organizations may need to dig more deeply into the major issues for their teams. As we include these topics in training, we will increase the value of our training for single members and enhance relationships with married ones.

One of the biggest issues that people wanted to see addressed in training is expectations. What is expected of singles? What do we communicate in our training about the policies regarding single and married people? Are we accurate in what we say compared to what is practiced on the field? Are we preparing them for a "baseball team," when in reality their team may be more of a "relay team"? Are we teaching about ideal team life as opposed to real team life?

Training influences what married and single people expect from each other in team life. Our training must include opportunities for interaction between married and single people; it should also incorporate communication between new people and the teams they will be joining. We lost count of the number of times communication was mentioned in the feedback we collected as a huge need and potential solution to team challenges! We must build opportunities for interaction in our training. Facilitating needed conversations around expectations is vital.

We can incorporate technology by requiring those joining our organizations to communicate virtually with their future teammates. Have a list of topics they are to cover so they can get a glimpse into their expectations of each other. Trust is built as we become vulnerable with one another and go deeper, being discontent to keep our relationships shallow.

The following questions are used by one agency to help teams take into consideration the needs of singles that might otherwise be overlooked. These "Questions for Singles and Their Team Leaders" were developed by a couple of single women after a painful experience on a team in which many of these things were missed.

Questions for Singles and Their Team Leaders

It goes without saying, but like any team member, each single man/ woman is unique, with different gifting and needs! This document has been developed by a couple of single ladies in the hope that it can help team leaders think holistically about their team member who is single.

Things for the team leader to think about/investigate *prior to* the team member's arrival:

TEAM LIFE
What team life is your team member anticipating?
Is this realistic?
How can they be included in team life?

LANGUAGE LEARNING
How will your team member learn the language?
Are they aware of their preferred learning styles?
How can you support them in learning the language?
Do you know of any good language tutors?

WORK
Can your team member use previous work experience to bless your team/ town?

SOCIAL
What does your team member perceive their social needs to be?
In your locality, are there other single people on your or someone else's team who your team member could socialize with?
Can you get their contact details?
Are there other single people in the region that you could connect your team member with either by phone/email/visiting?
How will you help them connect with the local community?

LIVING ARRANGEMENTS
What living arrangement is your team member hoping for?
Is this feasible?
How far away should they be living from other team members?

HOBBIES
How does your team member anticipate relaxing with hobbies?

Is that realistic?

Can you help facilitate that?

SPIRITUAL HEALTH
In what areas are your team member hoping to grow?

Can you support them in this?

What specific spiritual giftings does your team member have?

How can they continue to develop these whilst on your team?

What else would your team member like in order to stay spiritually healthy?

OTHER GIFTING/TALENTS/PASSIONS
What are your team member's gifts/talents/passions?

How might they be able to use them in your team/town?

How could they continue to develop these?

SINGLENESS
How does your team member feel about their singleness?

Have you affirmed their value as a single person on your team?

SCHEDULING
Considering all that you have discovered about your team member, have you discussed what their timetable might look like?

The statements in that sample were developed by single women due to their situation, but the same questions can be asked of single men. And we would hope that similar dialogue is going on with married men and women too.

Having single and married missionaries share their experiences when training those joining organizations is invaluable. The use of role-playing is recommended. The more interactive we make our training, the more effective it can be. One missionary said we need to "catalyze mutual understanding" among married and single members. We must create opportunities to learn from each other in the training we provide. Thinking through what we can do to foster teams should be at the forefront of our thinking about training.

And lastly, are married and single people treated and respected as equals in our training? Our training materials must communicate respect for the gift of singleness while acknowledging that many who are single may long to be married.

Even if our training has great preparation for singles and amazingly relevant case studies, we can dilute its effectiveness if we are not showing singleness the respect it is due as a calling of God. When we tease someone joining our agencies about a possible life partner also attending the training or about perceived romantic interest in one of their friends, we risk hurting our single coworkers. Lockerbie Stephenson points out the dangers of teasing, and warns men especially.

> Closely tied to the matter of letting friendships follow their natural course is the problem of teasing. Teasing is part of family life, but sometimes contains a barb. I have found husbands guiltier of this than their wives. Some men seem to need to say something about a single woman's getting married—or not. Be careful about flippant remarks. You don't know what the single you are talking to has gone through. You don't know the person or proposal she turned down so she could be where she is right now. You don't know if she is currently corresponding, weighing the issue: Shall I stay here and do this work, or shall I go home and marry him? Remarks spoken in jest can cause a lot of hurt. (2008, 63)

We are issuing a warning not only about teasing, but also unwanted matchmaking and the pressure it brings. One missionary told the story of a man and a woman who were friends. A leader in the organization noticed their friendship and encouraged the woman to look at the man as a possible life partner, not just a friend. She talked with the man, and though the friendship may have developed into something more, the event of asking for clarification about their friendship became the moment of its demise.

We must prayerfully consider the harm that can be done through teasing, matchmaking, and the underlying assumption that marriage is the best calling for everyone and singleness is less than marriage.

- Married people need to be very careful with their words.

- Single people need to be very careful with their words.

One way we all can do this is to listen well. We don't assume all singles or all marrieds are alike. We can ask powerful questions and actively listen. Our next chapter looks at communication issues.

Good Ideas and Helpful Tools

From a Survey Respondent:

"**PART OF OUR PREPARATION** was looking at the different groups (single, married, married with kids), thinking specifically about how each group is impacted on the field and hearing the thoughts of each group, as well as everyone's thoughts about the groups they are not in.... Excellent info and discussion."

From a Single Woman Working across Cultures:

Kat Moy, with a sister agency, shares the following concept she incorporated into the training her organization offers new personnel. After attending a Shoulder to Shoulder conference, she saw the need to teach a biblical theology of singleness and how it would help all missionaries and missionary teams to flourish.

"I started presenting an abbreviated version of Danylak's biblical theology of singleness. I also addressed the question "Why does this matter?" Once leaders started seeing the biblical basis and its potential impact, the training gained more traction.

My hopes were for others to see the foundation for biblical singleness. I also wanted them to understand how it could strengthen our teams and ministry. It would also help singles respond to common questions ("When are you going to get married?" or "Isn't it great you can do whatever you want when you're single?"). A biblical theology of singleness would encourage single people to embrace their singleness to the glory of God.

I would start with how other religions and worldviews view singleness. I would then compare those views with the incredible theology of singleness in Scripture. I also included practical notes of how useful this is for anyone to know in ministry, be they married or single. Those in the Muslim faith, for example, may give up marriage if they choose to convert to Christianity. Knowing how important family and cultural pressures are for these individuals, 1 Corinthians 7 can only address so much!

Even while presenting the theology, I tried to answer the "Why does this matter?" question. One of the most meaningful questions asked is this: If marriage is a picture of Christ and the church, what can singleness portray? Again, one of the goals is considering not only the inward affirmation that a single's identity is complete in Christ, but also to consider the potential impact as well.

Often books on singleness can focus too much on the inward and not on the outward. If the outward is mentioned, it is works-based. Knowing singleness can be a picture of eternal truths is much more powerful to me than hearing I have more time to work.

In the biblical theology of singleness, we see the prophets' marital status was part of their message. It is also a part of ours.

In his teaching, Danylak points out the differences in the ages:

- **OLD AGE**—everybody marries, the nation of Israel illustrated;

- **CURRENT AGE**—some people marry, Christ and the church inaugurated;

- **NEW AGE**—nobody marries, Christ and the church consummated.

I can't emphasize enough how important it was to cover it all with the question "Why is this important?" The goal isn't to make singles feel better about being single. Neither is it to give singles a reason to stay single or live purposeless lives—quite the opposite is true of that!

People wanted to hear about the vision and potential impact. They also wanted to know the theological foundation for it.

Application Question

- What are you willing to do to improve the training in your organization or for your team?

CHAPTER 5

It's Impossible to Over-Communicate

STATEMENT	MEAN
There is good communication between married and single people on my team.	Married 3.25 Single 3.07 *P*-VALUE .055

According to the survey, married people had a more positive view of the communication taking place between married and single people on their teams than single teammates did.

Suzy and I (Sue) were commenting on how many different forms of communication are available to us, yet communication still remains one of our top challenges! It is staggering to think that having more opportunities for communication has actually resulted in feeling less connected.

I remember the days before computers and smartphones or plain cell phones! I even recall the first CD player I ever saw. A teammate brought it back after his home assignment, and we all stood around the table and watched how it worked. I was amazed. I remember thinking that we would probably never have one of those! Needless to say, we did. Our family had more than one!

Back in the day, we wrote letters that took weeks to get to their overseas destinations. For conversations with family back home we only had expensive phone calls. Mailing pictures was so costly that we discovered it was cheaper to mail the negatives. We had monthly or almost no communication from our mission office. Today we have smartphones, email, Twitter, Facebook, Skype, FaceTime, Instagram, and texting. Expense isn't normally an issue except for the devices that we purchase.

By far, communication was the factor that survey respondents cited most frequently as necessary for healthy teams. Lack of communication kills team life. Poor communication damages team life. Effective communication enhances it so that team relationships can thrive. Communication isn't just words; it is also body language and how we say what we say. Our facial expression and tone can communicate more than our words.

Often when we are talking with others, we are only slightly listening because we are planning what our response will be. This is especially true when we feel strongly about our opinion. Because of the nature of our work and the eternal purposes of missions, we feel especially resolute about vision and philosophy of ministry. We want to be good stewards of resources; for some that means spending a lot, for others it means being frugal. We talk about it. A lot. We cling to our beliefs as we argue vehemently. Conflict ensues, and relationships are broken. We may have the same goal, the same vision, but the ways we want to get there can differ dramatically. What difference would good communication make when this happens?

Communication problems arise from the assumptions that we make about each other. Assumptions are suppositions—hypotheses that haven't been proven. They are ideas that we think are true about other people without knowing what is actually fact. If a lack of communication kills team life, assumptions are often the murder weapon! Jumping to conclusions without listening to others cannot have good outcomes. Both single and married people quite frequently mentioned assumptions as seriously dangerous in team life. Married people can assume that singles have a lot of free time since they aren't living with their family, and so they give single team members extra work without asking about their schedules. Single people may assume that married people are never lonely since they have a built-in best friend. So singles plan an event and do not think to invite a married person.

Single people might assume that a married person's sexual needs are always met. Any married person could lay that rumor to rest! Single people hear those who are married saying how busy they are. So why bother them with another invitation that would increase their busyness? They might assume that married people always feel blessed to have children. They are blessed for sure, but there are also challenges and struggles in raising children. When a single person wants to do something on the spur of the moment, he might assume his married coworker wouldn't be able to come. So the invitation isn't given; the married person might end up feeling a bit alienated and left out.

Married people might assume that single people have more adventures, more freedom to do things on their own. This is sometimes true, but not always. Married people might assume their single friends want to get married or would love to be fixed up on a date. This is not always the case. I assume that there is great freedom in not having to cook if you don't want to or letting dishes pile up if you want to. As a married person, what I do or don't do affects my family, and therefore I have to do things I might not want to do. I conclude that single people have more freedom to flex and to do what they want to do without consulting others.

What seems to occur between married and single people is that they see the best in each other's world and desire it for themselves: married people love the idea of freedom, and single people love the idea of companionship. But that is not the sum of a married or single person's life.

One example is a conversation that took place between a married woman and a single woman. Both people were speaking out of their desire and pain.

MARRIED PERSON: "My teenager is in rebellion. I don't know what all is involved. But my heart is breaking."

SINGLE PERSON: "At least you have a child."

The married person is sharing a burden that she carries as a mother. The single person carries an unfulfilled desire to be a mother and therefore offers no empathy to her hurting friend. She is consumed by her own pain and doesn't recognize that of her sister.

Or possibly there is a conversation like this:

SINGLE PERSON: "I'm not sure what I'll do this weekend. Friends are out of town. I feel a bit lonely. It is hard being alone sometimes."

MARRIED PERSON: "I wish I had that problem. I'm never alone!"

For the harried mother, time alone is precious and she is speaking out of her desire, totally missing the sorrow that her single friend is sharing. When we listen with self-interest, communication will not take place; barriers will be erected that hinder communication.

When we listen to others but are thinking only about our own hurts and needs, we do not minister to our spiritual family members. Caring communication isn't really taking place in conversations like these. The person sharing is not being heard, not being affirmed in his or her struggle. The person listening is not really listening, but rather speaking her own misery. Both are self-focused.

What would it look like if we took the focus off ourselves and took to heart the words of our friends? What if we responded with, "Wow, that must be difficult. I am so sorry. How are you handling the sorrow? What can I do to help?"

How often do we truly communicate with the other person's interests at heart? We often listen half-heartedly, assuming we already know what the other person is facing.

Numerous survey respondents shared their thoughts on assumptions:

"Don't assume. Encourage questions to help people understand each other. (Not all single people are lonely or looking for a spouse. Not all married moms want to be with their kids all the time.)"

"Relate to each other in terms of being brothers and sisters rather than in terms of marital status. Often so much trouble is caused because we see each other in statistical categories (married or single) rather than as individuals. Don't consider that either singleness or marriage is better. Listen to each other's 'personal' needs, not assuming that all married people and all singles are the same! Be really careful to not behave paternalistically toward the unmarried ladies on your team. They have made it all the way to a new country on their own. They need brothers and sisters, not a new father and mother!"

"Voicing expectations and legitimate needs and asking questions rather than making assumptions are so important for good relationships. Each person is unique and should never be stereotyped. Personalities differ and felt needs differ. For example, some singles like to do things together, while others [would] rather relate to others one to one. Singles are individuals, not a group."

"Sometimes there is an assumption that single people are all looking to be married, so constantly talking about romantic relationships or suggesting being set up gets old fast. Recognizing that being single is a choice I made, and [that I] actually can thrive and be content is rarely celebrated."

"Assumptions on both sides. We assume that we understand the needs and struggles of the other person, but often are mistaken."

There were many more comments about assumptions to choose from! Each of us must be intentional to ask and not assume what others are thinking. We need to practice active listening with one another so that we know and understand what the speaker is saying. We don't do so as we are planning our response, but we listen to comprehend what is being said, and in so doing we show value to the other person.

Communication gaps occur when people stop talking due to lack of forgiveness or previous awkward conversations. We think we know what the person will say and we don't want to hear it again, so we just avoid the person. Team members withdraw from each other, and the Christian love we are supposed to be modeling is tarnished.

When we send an email, what do people read between the lines? What do we communicate that we didn't mean to say? Can we truly build healthy relationships and communicate deeply via a text? What does good communication look like?

Here is a general rule of thumb regarding email and texts. If it's a sensitive subject or something you're quite upset about, do not use email or texts to communicate your concerns. If you are forced to communicate in writing, wait at least twenty-four hours to send the message, and give it several rereads to be sure the tone is one worthy of a child of the King.

It's best to work through relational issues and resolve conflict face-to-face or by phone, where we can hear the emotion in each other's voices and observe how our words are being received. This can help us in communicating serious concerns in more constructive ways.

Why would singles be less satisfied with team communication than married teammates? One possibility is that married people can discuss ideas before and after team meetings; single people often have limited opportunities to talk about issues outside of these meetings. We will take a deeper look at this in a later chapter.

Some good suggestions to alleviate assumptions came from people's responses in the survey:

"Give time to have an open discussion between all people of different marital statuses to know ... the struggles each one faces, and how to help meet the needs of people in different seasons of life."

"Ask, listen, be willing to go the extra mile."

"In general, assumptions and critical spirits are killers for team unity. This can happen whether people are married or single, but the marital status topic is one area it happens and we all need to be reminded that we are one body in Christ."

On the flip side of assumptions are expectations. Assumptions are thinking you know what another person is thinking. Expectations are thinking you know what the other person should say or do and waiting for that to happen. More often than not, expectations remain unmet. Unmet expectations occur more frequently when expectations are not communicated. Expectations was another major theme from the survey, so a later chapter is devoted to this topic alone!

How do single people expect their married teammates to communicate with them? How often would they like to touch base? What is their preferred method of communication? Phone calls? Face-to-face? WhatsApp? Texts?

On our team we have two couples and two single women. My husband hates getting WhatsApp notifications. We have a team communication WhatsApp group, which has the goal of sharing important information with each other. I considered an ice cream store reopening after winter newsworthy enough to share with that group. Others (just the women) were excited, and we began texting about it. Don dropped out of the group. In this group we share dinner invitations, team events, and local news. I have to tell Don about what is said because he doesn't want the "constant" notifications. He has no idea about how much more the women on our team text in our separate WhatsApp group!

We also have an emergency team WhatsApp group. Don tried to leave that one too, but I wouldn't let him! We never use that one unless it is a true emergency. And no, I didn't think the ice cream store opening was that important!

The other married man on our team wants to be in on the team communication WhatsApp group. If there is an invitation, he wants to receive it himself and not be told about it by his wife.

Different people, different preferences. It takes diligence to discover what means of communication is best for each person.

How do married people expect their single teammates to communicate with them? What time of day is best? Do husbands and wives each want to hear news or does one expect to hear it from the other?

When Suzy hears the same thing from a husband and wife, she responds to both to make sure they both hear from her. She gives this example:

> I got a call about nine in the morning from my team leader telling me about something he and his wife wanted to let me know about—an invite or something, and taking care of some team admin stuff. Then about an hour later I got a call from his wife. She proceeded to tell me the same things and go over each detail. I realized then they hadn't actually conferred with each other about who would call. I had to smile! I was thrilled they were both concerned that I not be left out. And it reminded me never to assume that couples pass along details to each other either.
>
> Actually, this has happened in one form or another with many of the couples on our field. I now make sure to copy both partners

when I send an email and never expect or assume one will tell the other. That way they both know. It's sort of the triangulation rule: generally best to go direct and not through others for best communication. That goes for couples too! *In the triangulation rule, directly communicating to each person honors both people, as they don't hear news from a third source.*

This is true! Once when my husband and I were talking with others, Don shared about an upcoming trip or event that I hadn't heard about before! Couples also need to communicate with each other!

What is the purpose of team meetings? Does everyone participate? Are those with introverted preferences drawn out so we can hear their voices? How does what was discussed get passed around to those who weren't there or to leadership?

What has been your team's pattern of communication? Odds are, communication needs to be improved.

When there are team meetings, is childcare provided? Nothing hinders adult communication like children interrupting with questions, fights, and diaper issues! Singles love the children on their teams, but they would also love some adult conversation so that not everything revolves around the children. Married people with children also get stressed when they feel alone in caring for their kids during team meetings. One person commented about this:

> I think it has hurt us, at least for our team. Since we are the only ones with kids, and the other married couple didn't do this stage we are in with kids, but adopted kids later in ministry, we feel like no one really understands us but will offer a lot of advice and opinions and just make silly comments that actually hurt us [rather] than help. And no one really helps us at team meetings to play with our kids or look after them or plan events that will be easy for us, with kids. Or if we do bring our kids, they won't help with them there. Things that they plan to be fun are meant for them, and end up being exhausting and stressful for us.

One married couple with small children was required to go to team meetings in the evening when it was their children's bedtime. Most of their teammates were single; this couple had the only young children. Their kids would be fussy that night and the next morning! The parents were tired after working all day. Would there be a better time for team meetings that would work for all? Could childcare be provided at this couple's home so their children could keep their routine?

How can teams creatively solve problems that affect members who are in the minority? Putting ourselves in each other's shoes can go a long way in improving opportunities for good communication! What are we doing to help foster communication on teams, especially during meetings?

It isn't just marital or parental status that can affect team communication. Suzy points out that personality also plays a role in team communication:

> One of the teams I was on took a look at our introverts and extroverts and how it affected our team. (There are many other styles of relating and how we're each wired that affect the team dynamic too.) We realized that up until that point the extroverts always had their say and the introverts contributed little. We discussed how this made us feel (extroverts dominating and introverts holding back too much) and how it hindered our team greatly. We decided that truly honoring one another meant the extroverts generally needed to listen and observe more and let the others talk first. By contrast, the introverts were asked to contribute at every level, and we allowed time for some ideas to "percolate" for them, saying silence was OK too. It wasn't a pressured thing.
>
> It was amazing how much we all learned from each other as we experienced that we all had valuable things to contribute—and we made space for that to happen.
> And the extroverts learned they didn't have to say everything! Repentance was needed on both sides!

Listening is one of the most important aspects of communication and a skill that we need to keep perfecting. We will take a deeper look at this in the next chapter.

Good Ideas and Helpful Tools

From Survey Respondents:

"**WE HAD A GREAT LADIES' MEETING ONE DAY.** The singles listed all the benefits and challenges for married women, and then the married women listed all the benefits and challenges for single women. Then we told each other what the truth actually is. Very insightful!"

(As Suzy and I talked about this, we thought this great idea could be broadened for men/women, leaders/followers, childless people/people with children, to grow in their understanding of each other.)

"**HAVE VERY, VERY CLEAR COMMUNICATION.** The couple on my team welcomed us to their house all the time, but let us know when they were having date night so that we wouldn't bother them those nights. The married woman on our team made it clear she couldn't always be the one cooking for team meals, so we took turns. Before we all came to the field we talked about our expectations for holidays and decided to spend them together."

"**THEY NEED TO DO WHAT MY TEAM DOES** ... talk about it. Talk about community in light of marital status. All the women on my team came together a few months ago and talked about what it means to be married or single on this team. There were four single women and nine or so married women. We talked about how we treat each other, whether we feel we have a voice, what makes us feel valued, what causes loneliness, etc. It was great. We went away feeling 'heard,' and sometimes that alone solves a multitude of ills."

"**CLEAR COMMUNICATION IS SO KEY,** as well as forgiveness and grace. We need to be listening to one another and making time for one another, even if this is not your gifting. And if there are needs, then there needs to be good follow-up to meet those needs. Don't just discuss the needs but then drop the ball and never follow up. We need to learn how to support and care for one another better. We have all put a lot of time and effort in getting overseas, so we want to make sure we are keeping our workers on the field and creating healthy atmospheres for them."

I HAVE PERSONALLY FELT FREEDOM on all the teams that I have been a part of. Of course, when my children were small there were times I was constrained; but I always felt a freedom to be who I was. Over the years, perhaps just maturing about and realizing that it's not all about me has helped me appreciate other marital statuses. Listening to singles share their struggles, barren women open their hearts, families talk of their heartbreaks over wandering children, married and single men admitting temptations, has opened my eyes and made me realize we are all broken vessels in need of Jesus. In our weaknesses we can allow his glory to shine. It will look different, though. And ... we do have so much in common, no matter what our status is.... . Let's talk about what brings us together."

Our Recommendations:

"In order to draw out introverts on your team, have a silent brainstorming time. Ask a question your team needs to discuss. Give people sticky notes to write on. Allot ten minutes for them to quietly write out their ideas and comments. Have each person share what he or she wrote. This gives the introverts time to process and allows the extroverts to think through their ideas more thoroughly before talking about them. More explicit instructions can be found at www.lucidmeetings.com/glossary/silent-brainstorming.

"Team leaders can send out an agenda before the meeting so people have time to think through issues that will be considered.

Application Question

• Who can help you improve team communication?

CHAPTER 6

When Hearing Voices Is OK

STATEMENT	MEAN
I take time to listen to each member of my team.	Married 3.28 Single 3.10 P-VALUE .048

Married people say they are more intentional about taking time to listen to each member of the team than single people say they are. We are grateful for their intentionality in seeking to listen well. In thinking about this, I (Sue) have come up with a few possibilities on why this might be so.

I wonder how boring my conversations might have been for my single friends when I was younger and had small children at home. How much did my talking have to do with diaper changes, potty training, getting up at night, feeling tired, trying to balance my time with ministry in and out of my home? I think my world was smaller than my single friends' world! Maybe other married people could relate more and would listen with more interest as we talked about similar issues. It is possible that single people get tired of hearing the same thing or know what we are going to say, so they don't listen or feel like listening as much!

It is also possible that married men, who generally hold more leadership positions, listen as part of their ministry description. As team leaders or field directors, listening is key to fulfilling their roles. Wives of mission leaders often find listening to others useful as they seek to help their husbands or lead in their own ministry roles. I would think single people in leadership roles would also seek to listen to those they lead. Roles could have a bearing on how much we listen to each other.

From the beginning of our cross-cultural ministry, caring for teammates has been a part of my role, but also a part of who I am. As a result, I've sought to listen. I think listening to teammates is important. Listening to the single people on our team is vital, as they usually do not have a built-in sounding board. But I also tend to be a talker, a born storyteller. So it could be (maybe probably?) that I talk more than I should and listen less than I think I do.

I recently discovered a startling factor in communication. As far back as I can remember, when people share a challenge or difficulty with me, I don't want them to feel alone. So I share my own story with them so they know that their situation isn't unusual or that they aren't the only ones who struggle in that area. It turns out that when I do that I take the focus off of them and turn it onto me! It actually detracts from their story and adds to my own.

I am learning that in listening, I should usually, if not always, keep the focus on them by asking more about their experience: "How did you handle that?" "What happened next?" "That sounds hard. How did God meet you there?" "Wow! What are you learning?" This helps them delve deeper into their challenge and how God is at work, and it keeps the conversation about them and their story. There may come a point when I can share my story, but not when actively listening!

There may be other married people (and single people—but we're focusing right now on married people, who say they listen more) like me who need to reevaluate not only how much they listen, but how they listen.

I have a single friend who longs to be married. This has been a major issue for her and she needs to talk about it, but she wonders if she talks about it too much. She wants to find the balance between sharing her longing and not wanting to always go there in conversations. She is afraid married people or other single people might grow tired of her talking about this. I appreciated her sensitivity and desire to talk about her need but not make it the focus of every conversation. If she talked about it all the time, people would not listen as keenly to her.

We can imagine another possible reason why the survey shows married people listen more to their teammates: Single team members might be more focused on ministry and relationships outside of the team. As a result, they don't see the need to listen as much to teammates. They are busy listening to others elsewhere. Team relationships might be secondary to them.

Suzy points out other possible explanations:

> I think others assume that couples hear each other out all the time. I wonder if singles feel they are not equipped to minister to couples who are struggling. We often hear that we can't possibly understand their pressures and struggles. An unwritten rule seems to be that if you're not married or don't have kids, you're considered less apt to be able to contribute something. This isn't true, but the message is sometimes there. I wonder if that doesn't hold some back. Sometimes we've heard so much about how overwhelmed some families are that we, as singles, fear we'll only add to their load. So we stay away.

Regarding the unwritten rule, young teammates of mine blessed me with their words and permission to speak into their lives as parents. Their words made me feel valued, respected, invited, and loved. They sent me this thank-you note for a baby gift I gave them:

Dear Suzy,

Thank you so much for "showering me " with your love and support. I can't wait for baby boy Bennett to wear his oh so soft newborn outfit, thank you! I can't tell you how lucky we feel, that even though our son will be far from biological family, he is entering into a wonderful family here, with a special honorary aunt in you. One of your responsibilities in this role is to be our mirror (and tell us) if we develop any parental blindness and lose sight in any way of what God has called us to do (you have permission.)

Love,
Erin, Ryan & baby

Maybe married people don't talk much to single teammates, so singles don't have many opportunities to listen to them! As a married person, I have benefited from the wisdom and life experience of my single teammates. I treasure opportunities we've had studying Scripture and praying together and their invitation to seek their insights into issues that concern me. What a loss it would be if I didn't ask and didn't listen to the hearts of my single sisters.

We must listen to each other. In *The Emotionally Healthy Leader: How Transforming Your Inner Life Will Deeply Transform Your Church, Team, and the World,* Peter Scazzero highlights the importance of listening for a healthy community: "We affirm and practice deep listening as an indispensable means of loving others well" (2015, 307).

Listening involves body language. Even when using Skype, it is important to have good eye contact and beware of our nonverbal communication. During a recent conversation, I was taking notes and wasn't looking at the person talking. She noticed and felt less heard.

Please put your phone away or turn it off. Nothing says "You don't matter to me as much as …" like taking a phone call or texting in the middle of a conversation with someone. If there are extenuating circumstances, explain this to them before the conversation begins. When my daughter's baby was due, I was having a conversation with someone and said before we started, "I am leaving my phone on vibrate in case my daughter calls. Her baby is due any time, and I want to be available to her." She appreciated knowing why I left it on. I ignored other calls or buzzes while we talked.

Very few circumstances should lead us to monitor phone calls in the midst of conversations. We are easily distracted. We can be a bit anxious. We aren't making the talker our primary focus.

In a survey I did of the women in our organization, being heard was one of their top-five needs. Though I haven't researched it, I think this might well be the case for the men as well. Listening is important at the team level and all levels of leadership.

Teams and organizations must ask their people if they are being heard and if they are feeling heard. Surveys should not be used too frequently. However, organizations could receive valuable feedback by surveying their members and asking how they can improve in listening and communication. On the flip side, when organizations send out surveys, it would be so helpful for members to fill them out! And if leaders ask if there is anything they could do to help communication, they must listen to the responses. Putting into practice some of the suggestions could improve mission morale as well as communication!

In the past few years our organization has tried "cascading information," a business-communication process written about by Patrick Lencioni in his book *The Advantage*. Lencioni describes it briefly in his blog at tablegroup.com:

> One of the most powerful tools for transforming any organization, whether it has fifty employees or five thousand, is a communication program that eludes most companies. I call this tool cascading communication—here is how it works.

> Members of an organization's executive team leave each of their meetings having agreed on a common set of messages that they will communicate to their respective staffs within a set period of time, usually between 24 and 48 hours after the end of the meeting.

> Then, members of their staffs communicate those same messages to their staffs, and so on until they have cascaded throughout much or all of the organization. While the depth that is reached by cascading communication varies depending on the size and structure of an organization, in most cases it manages to descend two or three levels below the executive team.

But what is important is that messages are being communicated consistently and quickly in a personal way.

After leadership councils meet in our organization, leaders pass on relevant information to those they supervise. Then those they supervise pass it on to others in their group. This was done to increase communication in our organization, since this area was highlighted as a weakness in an agency-wide survey. Sometimes people don't make time to meet to hear the news. And it could be that these are the same people who complain about a lack of communication. The fault can lie at both ends of the communication chain.

One of the side effects of not listening to each other is that trust is eroded. When we aren't listening to one another, we are quicker to point out another teammate's sin issue when it really is a personality or cultural difference. We judge more easily and relationships are more fragile when we are not listening to each other.

It might well be impossible to listen too much. We cannot over-communicate. Listening to each other is a good practice for healthy teams. We think resiliency is hugely connected to listening, to team communication. We also know that listening doesn't come naturally. It takes practice. We keep learning how to do it better.

One of the things I've been challenged with recently is listening to God. I come to him in prayer. I explain my needs to him, ask him for help, and thank him for what he has done. I basically do a lot of talking or writing in my journal. What would it look like for me to sit in silence and wait for him to speak to me? And if I develop this spiritual discipline of listening to God more, that would surely have an impact on how I listen to others.

Suzy talks about how meaningful it was when her leader took time to listen to her, but even more so that he listened to God and consulted with him about what Suzy wanted to do. It took time, but she felt heard and knew that his response was given after spending time with God.

Some years ago, I felt God was asking me to go to Australia to help our training team with a ten-day church-planting seminar. I'd checked with the training team and our Australian staff, and all were glad to have me come. As I was getting ready to talk to my field director and team leaders, I realized the dates meant I'd have to miss our annual field conference. "Uh-oh," I thought. It was clear they didn't want me to miss the field conference, and I assumed they would not "release" me to serve with the training team. But as we discussed it, my field leader looked at my team leaders and brothers and said, "I understand how we feel and why we want Suzy with us at our field retreat, but as I've prayed about this I feel like we're supposed to release her, and that God is in this."

I was so touched that he had talked to the Lord about it and went against what conventional wisdom told him to do. And that created the space for my teammates to release me too.

In the end, the training team had an emergency when one of the members had to fly home to his wife who was in a health crisis. Because I'd joined the team, we were still three people and felt we could move forward. The seminar would have been cancelled otherwise. Clearly one of those "God things."

What does it look like to listen to God as a community? How would seeking God together as a team, intentionally setting aside time to wait and listen to him, affect team meetings, discussions, and outcomes? I can't help but think there would be major benefits. We may have to work doubly hard if we have a history with someone who doesn't listen. If we are the one wanting to talk, we need to clarify what we need from the person we want to hear us. If we are the one who is listening to someone we've heard from regarding the same issue time and again, let's redouble our efforts to make sure we truly hear and understand where that person is coming from. As listeners, we need to keep an open mind, not having already decided before the person begins speaking.

But even before going the extra mile, might we suggest spending time seeking God together in prayer and fasting? Let's make each other an important priority. How can I listen well? How can I honor the person who is speaking? What would it look like to mutually respect each other in our communication efforts? How can we seek God together in this area?

Too often we withdraw. Listening or being heard seems overwhelming. We give up. Relationship gaps become chasms that evolve into abysses.

Suzy mentions that drawing people out is a huge part of listening. This is especially true for introverts and minority cultures on a team, who may drift to that quieter place. She believes this kind of listening may be the very thing that draws them into sharing more of their hearts:

I know I sometimes need to be drawn out or asked how I feel about things. Over the years, I've gone from being a clear extrovert to a closet introvert. Because I always used to share as an extrovert, I didn't always get to hear other people's stories. I no longer feel I must share my stories, but I wonder if some of this is because my stories are often the exception or might make others uncomfortable. Some sharing times can begin to feel like we're competing for who is busiest or has the hardest time right now. It was freeing for me, as an extrovert, to learn to wait and go last. If any extroverts try doing this they'll learn they may not get the chance to share at all, but that's OK.

We had a women's retreat on our field. It was an overnight gathering, and we had some great fellowship. The last three hours before we went home we had a dedicated prayer time where we all had to share something that was on our hearts that wasn't ministry-related. As we went around the room, the other twelve women present all shared their kid stories and we prayed for each one. I was going to share something about my singleness, but as I listened to all the kid stories I decided to share my own kid story about my nephew and some concerns I had for him. Even though it wasn't really the thing on my heart that day, it was just quicker and easier.

As I got in my car to drive home, I felt like the Lord grinned at me and said, "Nice cop-out back there." I laughed and said, "I know, but I really didn't feel like I had to make them enter my world. I guess I was just trying to enter theirs."

I didn't feel judged, just nudged to think about why I'd taken that tactic in the moment. It made me wonder, though, how many other women in that circle had something else on their heart, but just found it easier to follow suit.

If other agencies and teams are like ours, communication and listening need to improve. I don't think most missionaries generally feel that leadership is exceeding expectations in this arena. It seems that most teams would like to see improvement in communication. We all want to feel heard.

Good Ideas and Helpful Tools

HOW DOES ONE LISTEN WELL? Like anything we want to do well, it takes practice! Be intentional in listening to others. Ask questions to draw them out. Record a conversation. Review it, evaluating time spent listening versus time spent talking.

ATTEND a Sharpening Your Interpersonal Skills (SYIS) workshop (http://relationshipskills.com/syis/descrip/), where you can learn to love listening. Listening well is one way we can minister effectively to our teammates.

READ THE ARTICLE "Ten Steps to Effective Listening," by Dianne Schilling, at *Forbes.com.*

THE GREEN BALL A friend told me (Suzy) of an exercise she and her husband use when they are having conflict in their marriage and can't seem to get past the problem. They sit across from one another. They use a ball—it happens to be green! The one holding the ball begins. During this time, they share what they are feeling, casting no blame or criticism on the other. As they share, the other person doesn't speak at all. The person sharing talks until they've said everything they want to say. Then they toss the ball to the other person. That person then shares how they see things, again not blaming or attacking the other, and talks until they've said all they want to share. Again, the person listening is only listening (not thinking about how they will respond and not interrupting). Then the ball gets tossed again. They do this until they've talked it all out. Then they pray together about the situation.

My friend says that being able to fully talk and fully listen to one another really diffuses the situation, and it's much easier to move forward. I believe this same exercise could be used between teammates as well.

Application Question

- How will you and others be impacted if you do not become a better listener?

CHAPTER 7

Sounding Boards
Not Always Included

STATEMENT

I have a way to process information
after team meetings or from
mission leadership.

MEAN
Married 2.99
Single 2.75

P-VALUE
.035

More married people thought they had a way to process information after team meetings than single people did. It makes sense. Married people can more easily process things with their spouses. Sometimes, on a small team, it seems as if plans for the team can be formulated by a married couple without their teammates or even without a team meeting!

A few of the respondents talked about this:

"When there is interpersonal tension, married people have a 'live-in' sounding board that singles lack. Because of that, singles must sometimes 'blow off steam' with close single friends. While, technically, this might be considered 'gossip,' if done in a constructive spirit, it can provide necessary support and perspective."

"A team that includes one or more singles needs to be aware of the need singles may have for a sounding board. If a team is all marrieds, each couple has a built-in sounding board (although it is always helpful to have someone from the outside, as well, for a fresh perspective). Marrieds may find that they will need to be more intentional about inviting singles into their lives; singles may find that they need to be more intentional about making their needs known. All of this influences team dynamics."

"On our team, too, it seems like the married couples tend to think and express themselves very similarly—for example, my husband and I think similarly about team issues, and ... the husbands and wives of the other married couples, they tend to think similarly as well. At times the singles feel 'run over' in team meetings by my husband's and my perspective (expressed in double form!) or the perspective of one or another of the couples. As singles, it's hard to win an argument against *two* people, since you're on your own with your opinion. Of course, we try to be open and hear each other out, but I know the singles on our team have expressed frustration before that they can feel like the marrieds are ganging up on them."

With whom can single teammates discuss team information? Suzy remembers when she lived alone and there were no other singles on her team. Her teammates intentionally worked with her to ensure she had a way to process what she was thinking after team meetings.

I served on a team with two other couples. At one point we talked about how the couples tended to go home from the team meeting and process how things went. As a single, I might think about it a little, but I generally went on to other things after the meeting. As we discussed this together, the guys on the team made a decision to take turns calling me after the meeting to ask how I thought things went. It gave me an opportunity to process things in a way that was helpful for me and for them. This was a wonderful gift they gave me, and I feel it brought our team together even more. I hadn't even realized that I needed to be drawn out on how I was feeling about certain things. It also gave me a regular way to give feedback to the leader.

From what Suzy writes, it seems that singleness might not be the only reason she might not have a way to process information. It may also be her personality. Too often teams plan to move forward after only the thoughts of those with extraversion preferences have been spoken. They assume everyone is in agreement because some introverted people may still be internally processing. The team hasn't taken into account the thoughts and ideas of those who prefer introversion because they haven't taken the time to draw them out or to give enough time for listening.

I (Sue) am married to a person who prefers introversion. How much I would miss if I didn't wait to hear what he was thinking!

As teams, we need to know each other's preferences. We must take into account marital status, personality, life stage, energy levels, and life and ministry experience. Everyone needs a way to process team meetings.

Though it didn't show up in the survey, intentionally giving mothers of young children opportunity to discuss or process team information is also important. This is especially true if there is no childcare for meetings and the mother is in and out throughout the meeting. Having been in that situation, at times I could feel a bit disconnected and not "in the know."

How does your mission leadership make decisions, and how are they communicated? What decisions do teams make, and how are those passed on to mission leadership? One of the frustrations we have sensed in our leadership role is that we can hear from members throughout our organization about challenges they face; we seek to address those challenges, and when we come up with solutions that are implemented, they can appear as top-down decisions. In reality, these are bottom-up directed solutions. The problems might arise because of how we communicate or don't communicate about how and why decisions are made!

How often are we actively offering ways for our members to process information they are receiving? Emails are easy to write, and we are possibly too dependent on those in communicating. Writing about complex issues in emails doesn't seem wise. Talking face-to-face, or at least virtually, seems wiser. Skype, Zoom, FaceTime can all be useful when communicating internationally. We can too easily fall into a rut of using our preference for communication when we need to consider our teammates' preference.

What can we do to help our members process information? What will help them feel connected? What are our teammates' preferred methods of communication? What can married teammates do to facilitate their single friends' need to process team information?

It would be helpful for single teammates to state what would help them. What do they need to process the information shared at the team meeting?

Giving our teammates a way to process information is one way of caring for them. The next chapter will focus on caring for our teammates and seeking to meet one another's needs.

Good Ideas and Helpful Tools

Virtual town hall meetings My (Sue's) organization is introducing virtual town hall meetings to help members process information from mission leadership. The international director of Christar, Brent McHugh, sees this as a "next step in engaging our members about changes, developments, challenges and wins throughout the organization" (2018). This gives all a channel for giving and receiving information.

Conversation/Survey Teammates can put forth the effort to check in with single teammates and ask how they thought the team meeting went or if they had any questions. Teams could use an "after-meeting" survey or conversation after team meetings that asks the following questions:

- How did you think the team meeting went?

- Is there anything you didn't get a chance to comment on that you would like to weigh in on?

- What is unclear?

- What do we need to do as a team to follow through on what we discussed?

Teams could take a less formal approach by chatting over coffee after meetings to intentionally seek out those who might need time in order to process how the meeting went.

Application Questions

- What do you need to help you process information?
  - How can you get the help you need?

CHAPTER 8

Who Is My Neighbor?

STATEMENT

I seek to meet the needs of
others on my team.

MEAN
Married 3.21
Single 2.95

P-VALUE
.002

More married people than single people said that they seek to meet the needs of their teammates. Let's consider why that might be.

When we (Sue and family) were on a church-planting team, many activities and meetings took place in the homes of families. There were several reasons for this. Families' homes were usually larger than the singles' places, so there was more space for groups to meet. Also, due to kids' activities and schedules, it was often easier to meet in a family's home. Our places were usually more child-friendly. The kids had their toys, their rooms, their beds, which made it comfortable for them; and those things kept them occupied during meetings. When we hosted meetings, we normally had desserts and tea or coffee. Since I was already cooking for six people, adding a few more was easy—whereas for singles cooking for one, adding six or more to the mix increases the workload dramatically.

Also, do single people want children playing in their homes, possibly breaking things or getting into their possessions? I remember feeling nervous when going into people's homes that my children would break something.

Because we were used to hosting, I remember being very surprised and pleased when a single coworker invited us to his home for dinner. This was amazing to me, as it is quite the job to cook for six more people! He made some fried cauliflower, which I had never had before, and it was quite tasty. I told him how good it was and thanked him for making it. He said, "Well, we almost didn't have it, but God provided." I sensed a story behind that and asked him to share it.

It turns out he had the cauliflower, but was out of flour. He went to the store to buy some, but they didn't have any in stock. So he decided to go to the local bakery to see if they had some flour he could buy. They were getting ready to close and didn't have any either. But one of the bakers said, "Wait! In the back, where we knead the bread, there is still some flour lying around from when we were baking that I haven't cleaned up yet. I could just give you some of that!"

Our coworker thought that was a brilliant idea. He went in the back with the baker and wiped the flour from the counter and swept some up off of the floor (hopefully just the top layer of what was down there!). He put it in a bag and took it home to use for our dinner.

I remember being stunned, although impressed by his resourcefulness. And it really did taste good—although after he told us the story, I wondered if what I thought were spices sprinkled in the flour were really specks of dirt! The point is, he invited us to dinner. I didn't have to cook! I don't think I even helped with dishes! It was a treat.

This was the exception rather than the rule. I remember having people over for dinner often. We celebrated team birthdays and holidays. I wanted to be very intentional about meeting the needs of single people on our team because they didn't have their family with them. I think I saw my teammates as an extension of my family.

Singles may not invite families over as much as families invite singles, not only because they have smaller apartments but also due to limited finances. One time when money was tight, Suzy wanted to find a way to invite her teammates and their children to her place. This family was hosting guests from across the pond, so she invited them all to come by for a brunch buffet. She made things the kids would like, and there were lots of simple finger foods—but all in a more elegant setting. By not having a three- to five-course meal, it was more affordable, and the group didn't have to sit at Suzy's small table.

We may need to get creative in our hospitality, but we can enjoy fun times with teammates in our smaller places too. Any time all the burden is on the same shoulders, we're not practicing healthy care for one another.

One single teammate shared another aspect of showing care through hospitality in her survey response:

> My leaders have been great about inviting [singles] in as a part of their family! I greatly appreciate that. However, because they have kids, everything is done at their home, everything revolves around their family … and we just become a part of it. We are at their house all the time … but not once have they been to our house. Not once have they joined us. It's always us joining them. Again, I'm grateful for that … but would love to feel as though we were friends on equal ground—that, although they show interest in hearing about what's going on in our lives, they could actually be a part of it a bit.

When married people aren't willing to be a part of their single teammates' lives, everyone loses. Relationships that could have been enhanced won't be. Team relationships will become more fragile.

Making the effort to visit when invited to singles' homes or events is well worth the investment of time. Even if the invitations aren't there, we can find creative ways to invite ourselves. At a conference I attended there were discussion topics at different tables during meals. I really wanted to hear from my single sisters about their lives, joys, and challenges. After hanging back for a little while, I saw there was still an empty seat at their table and asked if I could join them. I wanted to listen so that I could learn more about their world. They were delighted to let me join! I benefited from what they shared. They seemed encouraged that I cared enough to invite myself to join them.

Since I could celebrate special occasions with my husband and my children, I didn't appear lonely. So maybe it seemed to our single teammates that they didn't need to regularly try to meet my needs. Maybe this is one reason that singles don't think to intentionally meet the needs of married people on their teams.

I do remember, however, one time when my single teammates took the initiative and came to the rescue. Our kids were probably around ten, eight, six, and four. Life was hectic. Ministry was hard. I am not sure what the warning signs were, but our teammates sensed we needed a break and treated us to a weekend away. They divided up our kids and took turns hosting them, playing with them, and feeding them while we went away together. It was amazing—just what we needed. We came back refreshed and energized. I felt cared for and ministered to. Someone took the initiative when they saw my need, and met it! I don't know which single friend came up with the idea, but I am so thankful that they did! I will never forget it.

That never happened again. (I might have tried to reenact the same scenario, but never got it right, as they did not offer again.) But I was so appreciative when teammates were willing to babysit. I didn't always expect them to babysit, but they did offer to watch our children if they could when we were in need. I appreciated that—and their influence on our children.

I recently discovered that babysitting can be a sensitive issue on teams. I remember people talking about it a long time ago, but I thought everyone knew we don't assume singles will always watch our children. Even today, though, many single teammates feel that they are expected to babysit.

One person gave this example:

Our organization advised married couples not to assume all the single women would eagerly anticipate being asked to babysit ... to basically be careful not to act on the assumption that as a single person, "Well, you have all this extra time on your hands ... " And I think that was good advice. In fact, perhaps the married couples took it all too seriously, being in two years I have only been asked to babysit on two occasions. But I think it's better, being a single of thirty-years-old, that I be very seldom asked— because then I can offer. And I have. I have offered to come over and watch the boys so the young couple can have a night off. And I would encourage other singles who have received the message of "I respect your time" from married couples on their team to do the same. Show your appreciation for the married couple that doesn't treat you like an on-call babysitter by offering to give them a night off once in a while.

Other responses from the surveys included:

"Don't ask the singles on the team to babysit or teach children's Sunday school. If singles offer to do that, fine. If they don't offer, that means they don't want to."

"Respect each other. To married people, include the singles in your family—and for more than babysitting."

"[It is hurtful] when marrieds see singles as opportunities to get free babysitting or childcare in church. If a relationship is developed, this can be appropriate; otherwise it feels that marrieds only value singles when they can get something from them."

"Sharing family life really helps. When a married couple has a single over for family dinner, sometimes it makes a big difference. Or if there are kids, [so does] the single spending time with the kids occasionally so the married couple can have time alone. (When there are kids on the team, I feel like it needs to be addressed up front that a single girl doesn't mean automatic babysitter—not to say she can't help, but don't just assume!)"

"Single women on the team would be expected to attend all meetings, whereas women with small children would be excused. Large group meetings, when everyone is present, often turn around the kids. I wonder how this feels for the singles or couples without children. Finding more common ground might help build relationships that all can enjoy."

If singles feel taken advantage of, they may be afraid to offer. Offering to babysit leads to an issue for some of our single brothers, who have offered to babysit and are not given the opportunity. One single male missionary loves children and would want to babysit, but he has never been asked. What is his role in missionary kids' lives? How can he be involved and not excluded? In many cultures single men may be looked at more suspiciously than single women. Team life might be the only chance he gets to be seen as an uncle and trusted with that role.

In light of the significant difference between married people and single people, what does this difference in views mean for single teammates? Are they not seeking to meet the needs of others on their team as much as their married coworkers? Have they tried and been rebuffed? Do married teammates think they are the only "official need-meeters"?

It could be that married people aren't vulnerable in sharing what they need from others on their teams. As empty nesters, we were new to our area, and I sometimes felt like I had no friends. I was lonely. I enjoyed my teammates, but those relationships were all fairly new; and I also wanted friends outside of my team. For a while I prayed very specifically for one friend from Spain and one friend from North Africa. After months went by, I crossed that off my list and simply wrote "friend." I remember praying as I did that: "Really, Lord, I just need a new friend. The only requirement is that she is breathing. I don't even have to like her!"

I shared my feelings of loneliness at a team meeting and asked for prayer. After the meeting, a young single woman who had recently joined our team said, "Hey, if you'd like to go get some coffee sometime, I would like that." We planned a time and met for coffee. (I won't go into detail about our adventure on the bus. It turns out we are both directionally challenged! That about covers the why of our adventure.) That was the beginning of a wonderful new friendship. After some time, I shared how much I appreciated her reaching out to me. She said she would have never offered if I had not shared my need. She saw me as an older, more experienced worker (which I am), but was mistaken in assuming that because of that I didn't feel lonely or had figured out how not to be lonely on my own.

Maybe, too, it is a matter of perspective. Do single people sense that married women seek to meet their needs, or do married people think they are seeking to meet the needs of others, but others don't feel it?

Suzy writes about an invitation she received from married teammates:

I got a call from a family on my field inviting me to come spend
the evening with them. On arriving we sat down to dinner, and
quickly after went into the living room to watch a movie. By the
time it was done I had to head home, as I lived about an hour
away, and their kids had to get to bed anyway. I went home
feeling something had been missing. I realize this had probably
been a fun night for them (especially with little ones). And really,
I'd been delighted at their invitation. They'd been so thoughtful
in thinking of me. However, as I drove home I came to see that I
had expectations of a more relational evening. I lived alone and
could watch a movie by myself in the dark with no interaction (as
we had that night). What I was missing was just time to talk and
laugh and have fun together—something I couldn't do on my own.

Our expectations can vary widely. We need to think about
what our "norm" is, and that will say much about our need. The
family with a hectic life with little ones may need a quiet evening
watching a movie in the dark. The single with a quieter "norm"
may long for face-to-face interaction.

I was invited back another time, and we played a game together
and had a blast! That met my need for interaction much more. The
kids still talk about that time, and I have a photo of us holding the
game box and making funny faces! That was over twenty years ago!

At least sometimes, when married teammates reach out to their single friends,
expectations on what makes it meaningful vary!

Quite a few singles made comments that show that their married teammates
weren't taking the initiative to spend time with them or seeking to meet their needs.

"I think married people need to spend time with the single person
as a couple, but also the person of the same gender should spend
time with them one-on-one sometimes so that they don't always
feel like the third wheel."

"I am often treated as the little sister on the team and spend a lot
of time watching other people's kids so families can do language,
have date nights, etc., but very little time with people on our team
besides church or team events. Even at team events there are
many times that I could sit and listen to a conversation, but have
nothing to say because it's all about family things. I definitely

appreciate learning from them, but it is easy to feel left out often. Because of all this, everyone else's relationships tend to be closer and friend-like, while mine is more coworker-like."

"I remember a single friend who was getting settled on the field and trying to get her apartment livable. She didn't have a car and she needed some heavy things, like paint. I was stunned to watch her mention her need to the couple who lived near her (and yes, they had a car). The couple told her there was a tiny hardware store at the end of her bus route! And there was no offer to help her do any of the heavy lifting on the bus, either!"

"From married folks, [there is] generally a closed attitude of 'This is my family and we do this with just us.' You are not a part of this family—never mind that you are alone at Christmas. Figure it out."

With varying expectations and different personalities, there are bound to be relationship hiccups, but having good relationships and growing in our understanding of each other is possible. One survey respondent sums it up well:

I think singles need to respect married couples and how couples need to have time to be with just each other; but married couples also need to realize that being single on the mission field is very lonely and can feel very isolating when you don't have good support and community from the married couples on your team. So I think both singles and married couples need to be open to having space from each other, but also open their homes/lives to each other.

Single and married people need each other. As teammates, we look out for each other. Married people do not have to always host. Single people can enjoy offering hospitality. Talking about our roles and needs helps! We must have open communication about what our needs are, sometimes being specific in that we need to get together to talk, not watch a movie or play a game. Or maybe we need to watch a movie and just enjoy being in another person's home. How do we reach out to each other? Can we talk about this as a team, because this will vary from team to team, from person to person?

Of course, we must keep in mind that we cannot possibly meet each other's every need. We weren't meant to do this! Only God can meet all of our needs. If we aren't looking to him and are being overly dependent on each other, we will end up disappointed and discontent with team relationships.

Teams need to intervene to help teammates when their host cultures devalue them. Our next chapter focuses on affirming our teammates when cultures don't.

Good Ideas and Helpful Tools

From Survey Respondents:

"I THINK IT'S VALUABLE TO TALK about how to support one another. What are everyone's needs? What do the single men/women need? What do the married couples and families need? I think a good talk about expectations, realities, and needs/hopes would help a team figure out how to thrive."

"MUTUAL RESPECT AND HONESTLY LISTENING goes a long way. Expect that you can support each other. It's not one-way. Expect that each person or family will have unique needs. It's not just 'single needs' and "married needs.'"

"LISTEN TO EACH OTHER and their needs. Each single is different and will have different levels of independence and resilience. Knowing what each other needs and being willing to help them find a sustainable life is very important."

"TEAMS SHOULD BE TRYING TO CREATE a family atmosphere as the body of Christ. They should be affirming each other's gifts, listening to one another, and if there is a need try their best to be available to meet that need."

"AT A MARRIAGE SEMINAR the teacher had each couple look at each other and say out loud, 'You are not the enemy.' This reminds them they are in life together, and many of the stressors and challenges are coming at them, not from each other. The enemy of their souls is seeking to destroy their relationship. At a team meeting this might be a good reminder when respect starts to wane and divisiveness reigns. Take a moment, look at each other, and say aloud, 'You are not the enemy.' This helps teams remember that together they are in a spiritual battle facing a common enemy who has already been defeated at the cross."

Application Question

- What steps could you take today that would improve ministry to your teammates?

CHAPTER 9

When Affirmation Gets Lost in Translation

STATEMENT	MEAN
The host culture I am in respects women regardless of their marital status.	Married 2.34 Single 2.06
	P-VALUE .021

More married people thought that their host cultures respected women regardless of their marital status than single women did. When I (Sue) served in the Middle East, I saw that if a woman was walking with her husband or with children the chances for harassment diminished. It didn't eliminate the possibility, but it did decrease the likelihood.

Ruth Ann Graybill, in her article about the emotional needs of missionary women, points out this need for women coworkers to be validated:

> The need to be validated tends to be even greater for those missionary women living in countries that typically devalue women. In Muslim countries, for example, where women are generally considered inferior to men, missionary women frequently report a stronger need for validation. Single women, especially, can find this a challenge in the Muslim culture. (5)

Married women are obviously not pursued for marriage. They are pursued for immoral purposes or possibly asked for connections to single foreigners. I remember, as I was waiting for a taxi one day, a local businessowner coming up to ask for my help. He said that he was looking for an American wife. He asked if I had any single friends who could marry him and help him with obtaining a green card. He would pay for their travel, and all he needed from me was the woman! It didn't fit in with my Western view of love and marriage; it was more of a business arrangement. He could get what he wanted: a green card. He could give the single woman what he thought she must want: marriage.

Many of our single friends received multiple marital propositions from strangers, relatives of their friends, and taxi drivers! Both married and single women received even more immoral propositions.

I don't think men can fully understand the vulnerability of being a woman in cultures that prey upon that vulnerability. Married women have some safety, as they are seen under the protection of their husbands. Single women who are living far from their fathers or older brothers can be seen as easier targets. Many have found it helpful for their fathers and brothers to visit so that they can be introduced. I have talked with some singles who regularly refer to their fathers when asked their opinions or questioned as to why they aren't married yet.

This lack of respect really isn't just about sexual harassment, though harassment is a huge issue. It is about being a woman where women are truly not valued. Their opinions don't count. Their work is discounted. Their roles are devalued. They are seen as a means to an end, not equals in life who deserve value and respect. In many cultures, married women are respected more than single women because they have achieved what those cultures deem as important for women—namely, marriage. Single women have not. Though singles may be respected less, the bottom line is that respect is often minimal for both.

I remember feeling extremely frustrated when traveling by taxi to a place to which I knew the best route. I was ignored. My instructions were discarded. The driver went the way he thought was best, and as a result we had to stop and ask for directions and it took much longer to get there. He assumed I didn't know the way—possibly because I was a foreigner, but more likely because I was a woman.

If we are working in a culture that doesn't affirm women, how might that be affecting team views of women? When we are seeking to contextualize, learn the language and culture of the people group with whom we work, it is very easy for their views and their customs to influence the ways that we live and interact. This is one of the fears that some missionary women face, according to Marti Smith, in her book, *Through Her Eyes*. Smith shares the story of one missionary wife who was fearful of the cultural effects on her marriage:

> "Because of the distance between men and women, I had this unspoken fear that it would affect Trent, and our marriage!" In other words, Vivian could picture her life becoming more and more separate from her husband's as he attempted to identify with and build relationships with men who had little interest in their wives' lives. "What was that going to do to our relationship? Was he going to abandon me or stop valuing our relationship in order to be more local?" (2004, 201-2)

When husbands are tempted to see wives as their servants or men are tempted to see women as sexual objects and not sisters in Christ, it is time to revisit our biblical roots and live counterculturally. If this can be an issue in marriages, it can also affect teams.

One way that teammates can affirm women, both married and single, who have been devalued by their host culture is to listen to their stories. In our attempt to help women learn ways to protect themselves from harassment, we often ask if they were doing something culturally inappropriate that invited the intrusions. This tactic can be perceived as blaming them and not the wrongdoers.

For instance, if a woman experiences sexual harassment and tells her team leader about it, the first questions asked should not be "What were you wearing?" or "Where were you?" This lays the blame on the victim and not the victimizer. Rather, empathy and statements that recognize the wrong that has been done should be first on our list. There is a time and place for learning about cultural appropriateness. That is not the time. It must also be stated that women can be doing everything right in the culture and still face harassment and devaluing treatment.

When one single coworker was slapped in the face by a taxi driver, we were all outraged for her. We listened to her, felt for her, were there for her. We could do nothing to the taxi driver, but we could be a support for her, listen to her story, and let her know the driver was wrong. We affirmed her right to ride in a taxi and pay an appropriate fare.

I (Sue) worked with a young single woman who experienced much pressure from men all around her. They greeted her, they wanted her phone number, they wanted to pursue a romantic relationship with her. It took time for her to adapt to the new culture, where she felt rude by her own cultural standards; but in her new culture what seemed like rudeness to her was interpreted as righteousness to those around her. She needed to learn to say no to those who wanted her phone number. She learned to not respond to taxi drivers. She learned to not eat lunch with men whom she saw as friends, because she realized they looked at her as a potential wife when she said yes. She was learning what she could do in her host culture to protect herself and her ministry.

I have shared quite a few stories about women in Muslim cultures, but women are vulnerable in all cultures, as Suzy illustrates:

> I have had some harrowing experiences in Paris, where I felt threatened or degraded, but certainly not at the level our sisters in some places have to bear. One of the bigger issues in Europe is the pressure of promiscuity. I learned quite quickly that what I

considered to be virtuous (purity) was frowned upon. I'll never forget the day three of my dearest single friends, who were not believers, came to me after I'd gone through a romantic heartbreak. They knew I was sad, and in their attempts to comfort me they told me they felt that the quickest way to get over this heartbreak was to "sleep around" for a while.

I was stunned. It was clear to me that they'd talked about this among themselves and decided I needed a "fix," and this was it. The conversation started out rather awkwardly, but I was able to challenge them on this, telling them that their own lives hadn't proven to me that they were happier or better off than I was. Yes, I was grieving, but I knew I'd be OK. God was there for me, and I didn't have the added baggage of a broken sexual relationship to make things worse. They all hung their heads and admitted that "sleeping around" may not be such a great fix. It was as though they realized in that moment that sex isn't the answer society claims it to be.

Another way teams can affirm each of their female coworkers is to encourage them to use their gifts, and to notice when they do. Be proactive in looking at the culture and opening doors for them to minister. If we limit women's roles and opportunities to serve just because the culture says they cannot, we are doing a disservice by failing to model and teach what Scripture allows and encourages.

As teams, let's have conversations about how our host culture views women. Let's talk about our different birth cultures, since those may well differ. Let's listen to each other's stories and experiences. Men and women need to be open to hearing what they are doing to devalue others on their team, as well as what can be done to show value. We can look at ourselves in light of Scripture. When we read about Priscilla, Aquila, and Paul, how do we see them working together? Reading through Paul's comments about his coworkers in Romans 16 shows us the value he placed on men and women coworkers, and he communicated that value in writing!

For mothers who are homeschooling and feel like second-rate missionaries, can we not affirm their roles in helping families stay overseas where educational opportunities are limited? Can we show gratitude for their role in discipling the next generation?

I was asked to speak to a group of women in South Asia on the importance of their roles as wives and mothers. Some were believers; some were Hindu. As I shared about the vitalness of their influence on the new generation and thanked them for their contribution to society, one woman in the front row wept. She said that no one had ever told her that before. She was working to provide for her family; she was raising the next generation for her community; she fought tirelessly for her children to get a good education. She did it all while feeling invisible and unimportant to those around her who only saw a mere woman. No one recognized her worth.

No one.

How many missionary women feel the same way as this dear woman? As a mother balances ministry roles in and out of the home, she can feel that her work in her home is not as valued as the ministry outside of her home. Let us affirm her contribution in the home. Let us also equip and encourage her as she seeks to minister outside of her home, recognizing her time and family limitations. As her children grow, her opportunities outside the home will increase. Let's keep dialoguing and thinking through ministry objectives and how this plays out in different seasons of life.

And what about the single moms and widows who are carrying the burden of parenting alone? Do we come alongside them? Do we listen to their struggles? We must affirm their unique value to God's kingdom. It's amazing how far our little offerings can go in showing care for one another. Are single women and married women without children valued for their contributions? We must learn how to celebrate spiritual motherhood and be more sensitive to the different seasons of life spiritual mothers experience.

Suzy has been deeply impacted by the idea of spiritual motherhood.

One of the great shifts in the New Testament is the shift to the emphasis on spiritual family. We are all given the task of making spiritual children and advancing God's kingdom. This mandate is the great equalizer. We are all called to do this, whether we are married or single, with or without children; young or old, rich or poor. This is our mandate until Christ returns.

Over the years, people have introduced themselves to me and asked how many children I have. While I'm secretly delighted they think I could be married with children, it creates an awkward moment. I used to hang my head and mumble, "Oh, I'm single and I don't have children." Then we both felt bad. But now I answer differently: "I don't have any physical children, but I have many spiritual children and even some spiritual grandchildren." This combats a possibly awkward situation with truth and makes people curious.

The Bible contains many stories of women in all different situations. God used married women, single women, prostitutes, foreigners, old, and young for his purposes and glory. However, in the world there are both spoken and unspoken messages that can contribute to the lies or truths women believe about themselves. Grieving with those who grieve and rejoicing with those who rejoice can show our love to those in different places in life than us. The team must figure out creative ways to love and value their sisters that honor God and challenge the status quo.

We need our dear brothers to step into our lives and affirm our value in Christ, as married or single sisters. (Women have the privilege and responsibility of affirming their brothers as well, as we discuss in the next chapter.) As sacred siblings, we have an honored role as we preach the gospel to one another in the best and worst of times, and nudge each other back to him often. We can't fix every problem or difficulty inherent to our parental, marital, or gender status. But surely living out reciprocal care and respect for one another is part of the great witness the church is intended to proclaim. How else will those we are trying to reach understand what Jesus is like?

Suzy recalls:

> I remember moving to a new area to be part of a new church plant. The team I was on understood that we were the church in that place already and that how we treated each other would bear its own fruit. We also made an effort to connect the people we were getting to know with others on the team so they could see we were part of something bigger than ourselves.
>
> Much later some of my single friends became interested in spiritual things, and a few eventually came to Christ. They said that one of the things that drew them to him was how the men on my team treated me and cared for me. They were watching, and it spoke volumes! Another friend told me, "I think people are in relationships for what they can get out of it." That's why seeing something different caught her attention. They'd never seen healthy brotherhood and sisterhood lived out in their midst. Our impact on lost communities is greatly enhanced or diminished by how we love, value, and treat one another.

Women were created by God for his glory. As gospel-bearers and kingdom-minded people in cultures where their personhood and value are questioned, we must teach and model their value to him as his creatures.

One thing we also want to point out is that we heard from single men missionaries about this issue as well. They said that they would gain more respect in their communities, and sometimes in their mission organizations, if they were married. It isn't that they are necessarily devalued in their culture because of their gender, but rather because of their marital status. They aren't seen as grown up or mature until they are married. Single men, especially those who are older, are not as esteemed or affirmed as their married brothers—although they might, in reality, be more mature or wiser! If they are single, it is assumed that they aren't ready for leadership yet.

Several years ago, a few single missionaries were listening to Cambridge scholar Barry Danylak share his work on the biblical theology of singleness. All were deeply impacted by ideas from the stories of the barren woman and the eunuch. Here is a brief summary of the two points Danylak makes:

> Unlike the Sinai covenant, in the new covenant barrenness is not a sign of reproach or disobedience. Single persons, whether "eunuchs" by birth, social convention, or personal choice, are no less blessed as participants in the new covenant than those with the sweetest marriage and a "quiverful" of children and grandchildren. (2010, 144)

> But in the aftermath of the work of the suffering servant, both the barren woman and the eunuch are blessed. The barren woman, who was unfruitful in producing physical offspring, is now able to bring forth something profoundly greater—spiritual sons and daughters in the pattern of the servant. Her legacy of offspring is even greater than the fertile woman, since the Lord himself is her husband. The eunuch, conversely, who had been denied access to temple service, is now given an eternal and permanent place within God's house. Instead of being a figure of reproach, he becomes the model of uncompromisingly loyal and devoted service to the Lord in the pattern of Daniel the prophet. In his inheritance within the walls and house of the Lord, he shall inherit a legacy and name even better than sons and daughters. (ibid., 117)

After reflecting on these truths, one of the men present, a thirty-six-year-old seminary grad who was working in Eastern Europe on a Muslim ministry team, shared the following:

> I'm not against marriage. In fact, God may one day ask that of me; but for now I know he has called me to minister to Muslims. I fully expected some complications with the Muslim men I am working to win to Christ. They do not understand singleness, and they are always trying to find me a woman. They can't imagine how I can live without sex. I was prepared for this. I knew it would be tricky, but I've

seen God use my testimony as a single man in their lives. What I was not prepared for was the pressure I would feel from my married teammates. I just wish they could learn how to encourage me, without encouraging me to marry.

Both men and women need affirmation in their calling as single or married people. But as we have been looking specifically at what single women face, here are some excellent suggestions from our survey respondents about the help they received from their teams:

"[Our] host culture expected singles to marry early. Our team understood this, but made it clear that singles were fully accepted by God and others regardless of marital status."

"One day, my team leader said to me that he recognized it must be very difficult for me to be here as a single woman. That comment meant the world to me. It is difficult, and I really appreciated his seeing this for what it is."

"Our team is very good at honoring each other and the gifts that God has given us. There is a need to honor the culture [as well], and our team has been very good to do both."

"For singles in our culture, we just need to be supportive when the culture beats them down for not having gotten married 'yet.' It's really important to encourage and build up when they are beaten down by this cultural expectation."

"Males often take on the role of brother to clarify honor and respect to [the] host culture."

"I think [my teammates] go above and beyond to counter the cultural norm in reference to singles."

Lastly, one person shared:

I think we made some pretty lame rules for our singles that may have not been necessary, that were dictated by the culture. I think if we had been truly demonstrating brother/sisterhood, then the culture would have seen that we were different and not made the assumptions we were so worried about.

It is this brother/sister type relationship we would love to see developed more on our teams in the countries where we serve. We've been using the term "sacred siblings" a bit in our writing. In the next chapter we are going to delve deeper into what we mean by it!

Good Ideas and Helpful Tools

Teams welcoming newcomers should have a thorough orientation intro-ducing their host culture and exploring its views on women, both Western and local. What is seen as offensive? What is considered respectable? What can a woman say/do/wear that will help the community see her as righteous? Prepare women new to the field, who may do everything correctly but still face harassment.

Offer regular debriefing for the women facing constant harassment. Encourage them to read Sue's blog post on "When Harassment Meets Forgiveness" (2017) to help them think about forgiveness in the midst of the challenges.

WE HAD BEEN LIVING IN THE MIDDLE EAST for a while and I knew culturally what was proper and what wasn't. I knew the language. I knew how to deal with sexual harassment. It was appalling, but also expected, since it was so common. Dress modestly. Don't look unknown men in the eyes. Don't talk to the opposite sex in public. Keep conversation with taxi drivers to a minimum.

I was fortunate in that when I was with my husband, I rarely had trouble. Having children with me was sometimes a deterrent to the less aggressive harassers. When I was out and about in the city, I grieved that I had to prepare what I would say or do when touched or spoken to inappropriately.

Sexual harassment was rampant. It shriveled my soul and made me feel unfortunate to be a woman and ashamed at what men were like. I came to detest and judge men I didn't even know as I saw each one as a possible predator.

What angered me, though, is that I could do everything right in that culture—according to *their* rules I was doing what should protect me as a woman—and still be hassled. In my dress and my behavior, there was no cause for harassment of any kind. Yet, it still happened.

And in their culture, I was the one to blame. Not the men. I discovered that women, though veiled and covered from head to foot, would continue to be an object of sexual interest and still be at fault for arousing that interest. I learned that when a woman is harassed, she is to blame. She bears the responsibility. Men are free to continue pursuing evil.

There were socially acceptable, and often effective, responses to harassment. I could ignore filthy words though they still pierced my heart and dismiss lewd gestures though they offended my morals. Seeking help from others nearby was an option. I once asked an older man for help and I can still see him chasing the young men away with his upraised cane. Other options included praying for protection and resorting to a physical response such as hitting or punching. Though not encouraged, it was sometimes necessary. In seeking to protect myself and a friend, I had no recourse but to swing a fist at a young man who unfortunately (from my perspective) or fortunately (from his) ducked and I missed. There were phrases to shout to shame him such as, "Don't you have a mother or a sister? Would you want them treated this way?"

Time after time, year after year, there were episodes of harassment. After every unwanted touch and unwelcome proposition, I felt a little less pure, a little less whole each time.

It came to a climax one afternoon when I was walking down the street doing everything that was culturally proper. From a distance, I saw that there was a man walking toward me. I was modest and looking down, not planning to say anything. Moving away to the other side of the walkway, my goal was to avoid any encounter. He veered toward me and made an obscene gesture, impossible to miss.

Angry, I said, "God damn him to hell," as I evaded him and hurried away to get as far from him as possible.

Did I pray those words? Was I asking God to condemn him? I think so. It was as if all those pent-up feelings of helplessness and rage came bubbling to the surface. I hated this man so much that I wanted him to suffer everlasting agony apart from God because of his wicked behavior toward me.

I didn't get far before I seemed to hear God whisper, "Is that *really* what you want? Do you want this lost man to spend eternity in hell?"

"Yes, that is what I want." I thought.

And then I thought about what hell is like. Eternal punishment. What it would be like apart from God—forever in torment, in agony, in darkness away from the light and love of God. I reflected on my sin and what I deserved because I am a sinner, too. My destiny was that same eternal destiny until God in His mercy saved me.

I realized anew that if it wasn't for the grace of God, because of my sin I would also be doomed. God forgave my sins through Christ and I could now spend eternity with Him. What if I had never met Jesus? What if no one told me about His love for me? I, too, would stand condemned.

In that moment, I knew I could not wish upon a fellow human being that eternal punishment. And by God's grace I forgave that man. I prayed that God would not hold that sin—aimed against me—against him. I prayed for his salvation, that someone would tell him about Jesus.

That forgiveness didn't change my circumstances; it was not a one-time event that changed my heart forever! Yet, forgiving and continuing to forgive, kept *his* sin from poisoning *my* soul. I still went out of my home prepared for possible harassment and struggled in my attitude toward men in that culture. I was angry at the injustice for women in that place and still am.

Forgiveness didn't condone his actions nor excuse his behavior. It didn't mean that if there was a way for him to be accountable for his wrongdoing I wouldn't take it. In some parts of the world, women have recourse. They can take legal action, go to the press, report it to the police or their employer. In many of the countries where women go to share the gospel, this is not the case. These women do what they can to protect themselves and others. Teammates seek to be of help. The community can come to her aid. But, for the sake of the gospel, they encounter unwelcome touches, rude comments and immoral propositions. They do so knowing it will continue to happen until communities are transformed by the gospel they came to share!

I want to acknowledge their hardship, affirm their ministry, and pray for their protection. I pray that God will shield their bodies from harm and their souls from bitterness. As they live godly lives, in the midst of darkness, may their light shine in the name of Jesus. May men and women come to know the forgiveness found only in him. May harassment stop and respect be given as God changes lives.

I recognize there are women who have experienced far worse than harassment. Young men face predators. Evil people extort the weak; exploiting children and marketing slaves. It is heart-breaking that people sell other people. It is soul-wrenching that people buy them.

I long to see injustice in this world stopped. I hope to see evil punished and justice come. May mercy flow and the vulnerable find protection.

Let us pray for all souls, those who are wronged and those who perpetuate the wrongs, to know Jesus. He is everyone's only hope for this life and the life to come. One day God's wrath will come. Injustices and evil will be punished.

Until that day, may we each experience that amazing grace where we find forgiveness of sins in Christ. Out of that grace, may we also forgive those who hurt us and seek to protect those who are yet vulnerable.

Teams can brainstorm statements of affirmation, and each team member could choose three that would be meaningful to them. Teammates can be intentionally aware of using those when appropriate. Being specific with affirmation is necessary. "You are appreciated" is nice, but it doesn't mean as much as when someone says, "I appreciate how you helped us think through next steps in our ministry project!"

In the team's desire to contextualize with their host culture, be cognizant of biblical mandates that should not be changed when adapting to host cultures. Where there is prejudice against another race, bias against women, injustice toward the poor, or mistreatment of children we must stand firm in the truths of Scripture and live out that truth.

Application Question

• What might change how affirmed the women on your field feel?

CHAPTER 10

Sacred-Sibling Relationships: Living Counterculturally

STATEMENT

Women are seen as sisters in Christ by the men on my team.

MEAN
Married 3.73
Single 3.53

P-VALUE
.007

MEAN
Female 3.58
Male 3.77

P-VALUE
.021

STATEMENT

I am seen as a perceived threat to the marriages of couples on my team.

MEAN
Married 1.00
Single 1.13

P-VALUE
.008

MEAN
Female 1.11
Male 1.00

P-VALUE
.037

Technically, "I am seen as a perceived threat to the marriages of couples on my team" should be in the next section of the book. However, because of its relevance to being seen as a sister in Christ, we are keeping it in this chapter.

Married people were more likely than singles to feel that the women were seen as sisters in Christ by the men on their teams. But interestingly, there was also a significant difference in what men and women thought about this. Men were more likely to feel that the women on their team were seen as sisters in Christ than the women. This is a disconnect.

In addition, more single people than married people felt they were perceived as a threat to the marriages on their team. This was also more of an issue for women than men. Single women on some teams feel that they are seen or treated as possible threats to their married teammates. Married people and single men don't think it is a problem. This is another disconnect. To gain a better understanding of how different groups understand sisters or issues pertaining to treating women as sisters, we've included some comments from survey respondents.

Here are some comments from our single brothers about team life for them:

"It has always felt a little uncomfortable to me to develop and deepen relationships with the girls on my team. Maybe it's good that it stays pretty high-level, but I wish there was an appropriate, safe way for it to go deeper."

"It is just a struggle when you are the only single, young male in the team and wherever you go. No matter how extroverted one may be, there is a sense of accountability brother/sisterhood we need. That has been the hardest struggle. So many times, I see myself drawing away from team time and rather wanting some time with other single people."

"I think it's good if people are comfortable with one another. I feel no weirdness when I get coffee with the female single on our team, despite having a girlfriend. Nor do I feel any weirdness with the wife of the family with whom I live. There is an aspect of trust that makes me feel comfortable. If their marriage was on the rocks, I might feel differently about it, but I believe it is at a level of health that allows for this dynamic."

Our single sisters shared some of their struggles and joys relating to men on their teams:

"Fear of moral failure. I think if we would concentrate more on cultivating a brother/sister relationship, we would have less fear of this. Instead of unspoken fears, we should address them openly. The old standard of not riding in a car together often gets in the way—I would ride in a car with my blood brother."

"It can be very hurtful and excluding when married couples always sit together, and even ask singles to move places in order for them to sit together. In team activities, we should be siblings first."

"It can be very difficult to have friendships with the men on the team until I can convince them that I am not a threat. Men really need to learn how to be our brothers."

"There is a sense of awkwardness from some of the married men, when in reality no one is really attracted to them; the singles are just trying to find a place where we belong. Just because we are single doesn't mean that we are going to fall in love with any married man [who]says hello to us."

"I appreciate that my team leader still gives me a hug as a woman. Some men wouldn't do that, but I feel more like family and loved/welcomed into his family and team because he's willing to do that."

Purity

We guess there may be some vixens or Romeos in the mission population, but we think we can safely say that cross-cultural ministers are not out to take anyone's spouse away. Most do not fit this category! They want to love Jesus, serve him, and go to areas of the world where he is not yet recognized so that others can know him too. Men and women can serve together in honorable ways.

Marriage does not protect you from immorality, and being single does not mean you are more likely to be immoral. It is a purity issue for all of us. Barry Danylak often says there is no big difference between him, as a single man, and a married man when it comes to purity. He is to abstain from sexual relationships with about 3.5 billion women, whereas a married man must abstain from 3.5 billion women minus one. Somehow, we think that married people are more protected from immorality than single people. We are all susceptible. And we can all be empowered by the Holy Spirit to live in purity.

In the apostle Paul's second letter to Timothy, his young disciple and growing leader, he wrote: "Flee the evil desires of youth and pursue righteousness, faith, love and peace, along with those who call on the Lord out of a pure heart" (2 Tim 2:22). No one who loves Jesus and seeks to serve him wants to fail morally. And yet it seems that we're constantly hearing about well-known, effective ministry leaders who do just that. What does that say about normal us? If it can happen to them, it can happen to us. What chance do we have? Others must think like us, because it seems that in our strategies to flee evil desires, we have plans and are proactive in trying to protect ourselves and our teams.

Many agencies recommend or require filters on their members' computers and other devices to help them not get trapped in viewing pornography. Covenant Eyes (www.covenanteyes.com) provides one such filter; people who use its services find accountability partners to help them flee evil desires. Most are aware this is a common struggle for men, but it is increasingly becoming an issue for women as well. Fleeing impurity in what we read, watch, and think about is essential.

There is the "Billy Graham rule," where a man is never alone with a woman other than his wife. In addition, some cross-cultural contexts also dictate that a woman must not be alone with a man. In cultures where reputations can be won or lost based on a male/female conversation on a public street, we have to be even more diligent.

I (Sue) remember a story that shows the severe consequences of crossing, even unknowingly, local customs. When we first joined our organization, there was a young family who had to leave their first ministry assignment in Central Asia. Why? Because a man came to see the husband, who wasn't yet home. Seeking to be hospitable, the wife let him in because she knew her husband would be home very soon. Children were home. Nothing happened. There was no desire for anything to happen. Her husband came home soon after. But her reputation had been ruined by a simple act of hospitality because of assumptions made by her host culture.

We must know the culture where we live and adapt to some cultural norms in order to build bridges into new communities. Teams can develop guidelines to help us maintain good reputations in our host cultures. We talk about public interaction between the sexes, what to do if a spouse isn't home and someone stops by, what touching or not touching is culturally appropriate, and things like that. Men are extra careful in thinking through their responses when single coworkers need assistance. What time of day is it? Will anyone else be there? What will neighbors think?

These things are all good to consider, and we must be proactive in thinking through cultural implications. However, when local culture dictates how we respond to women, it almost always comes at the cost of single teammates. When teammates decline to help or don't take the time to creatively think how they can help in culturally appropriate ways, single women lose.

In seeking to protect reputations and maintain a gospel witness, we have focused so much on the aspect of fleeing evil desires that we probably haven't sufficiently pursued the positive things Paul wrote about. In our relationships, how are we pursuing righteousness, faith, love, and peace? How can we refuse to settle merely for fleeing but actually pursue righteous, loving friendships? Indeed, not just friendships but the sacred-sibling relationships that Sue Edwards mentions in her book, *Mixed Ministry:* "Men and women really can be friends. In Christ, they can be more than friends—they can be sacred siblings, and the implications for ministry are enormous" (2008, 22).

One of the survey respondents shared this with us, which supports the sacred-sibling mentality:

> I have recently discovered writings by Joseph Hellerman, *When the Church Was a Family* and *The Ancient Church as Family.* He describes how the Jewish community considered the brother/sister relationship to be the strongest. And so when Jesus made the startling statements about who were his mother and brothers, he was reshaping the true family to be the family of faith, not the nuclear family. Very challenging.

But what about temptation to moral failure? What about cultural bias in communities where we serve? We have sometimes been so quick to adapt to the cultures where we minister that we haven't thought through the biblical example we want to set forth in contrast to our host cultures.

What does Scripture teach about male and female relationships in the body of Christ? Edwards addresses this as she looks at how Paul viewed the community of faith:

> Paul insists that we see the opposite sex as family members first, not as sexual objects. God considers lust between a biological brother and sister to be abhorrent (Lev. 20:17). Just as sinful is lust between any man and woman, according to Jesus (Matt. 5:28). Shouldn't it be unthinkable to lust after a spiritual brother or sister? Followers of Jesus are to consider one another as family, as sacred siblings. Is this mission possible? Are we able to see one another this way in the family of faith? Yes, God enables us through the power of the Holy Spirit working in our hearts and minds to love one another as siblings. How might churches be changed if men and women caught this vision and lived it out? (ibid., 26)

How can we model pure relationships as brothers and sisters in Christ? Avoiding relationships with the opposite sex is a popular way in some mission circles, but what does that say about the power of God and the value of each other in the body of Christ? If single women are ignored, how can that be helpful and what does it assume about women?

In the Middle Eastern culture, where I served, women were seen as weak creatures who could not control their physical desires, so they had to be chaperoned and contained in their homes. One hint of a scandal, whether they were innocent or guilty, could cost them their lives. Guilt was assumed so that honor could be maintained. When cross-cultural workers avoid their sisters in Christ, isn't that compounding an already negative and derogatory view of women?

Edwards quotes John Ortberg in regard to the struggles of developing pure relationships in the midst of oversexed societies. Ortberg also is explaining the weakness of an unbiblical "strategy of isolation" in churches, but I think it applies to missions as well.

> I think too often churches either avoid the topic or settle for an unbiblical "strategy of isolation" where men deliberately separate themselves from women as a means of temptation avoidance. This leads to a loss of biblical community, lost opportunities for the development of leadership gifts, and doesn't even help in avoiding sin. For God's intent is that we aim at becoming the kind of persons who treat one another as brother and sister. (ibid., 28)

We love the concept of sacred siblings. As brothers and sisters in the Lord, how are we loving and serving one another? What are the hindrances to this concept?

When married people are feeling insecure in their relationship, jealousy can become an issue. Jealousy prevents them from helping sisters in Christ, and this can put a burden on single women that they shouldn't have to bear. If a husband or wife is overly jealous and sensitive, it is his or her issue—not the single teammate's. Yet she is the one who suffers for it and feels the brunt of being perceived as a threat.

We are not talking about extreme situations, in which there is obviously a problem. People are so afraid of those situations that we fail to help when we could! Married couples must get the help they need. They can seek strategies to build trust; and they can talk about how trust is lost or has been lost.

What do wives need to know or do to build trust in their husbands and their teammates? What is fearful imagination, and what are certain trust-breakers? Husbands and wives must develop strong relationships with their single teammates to build trust on all sides.

One of the men who participated in the survey expressed his struggle with wanting to help single teammates, but feeling limited:

As a man, I feel a need to protect and comfort. I want to be there for my single teammates. I want them to be able to call on me when they need to. I'd even like to give them a strong, comforting hug when they need one—like a brother. However, as a married man, I feel like I can hardly do any of that—especially as my wife is maybe more sensitive than others about that stuff. (She doesn't want me to give them a ride into town without someone else with us or be in their house for even five minutes to help with something). I also do understand that I (we) need to be careful—things often start "innocently." So it's just hard, and I don't know the answers.

The onus isn't only on the husbands. The pressure isn't just on the wives. What can single female teammates do to help build healthy relationships among the sexes? Several mentioned the importance of building strong relationships with the wives.

One single female leader wrote about her experience and the importance of developing relationship ties with married women on teams:

As a single woman in leadership, I realize that I need to be very aware of my role and my relationships with the others with whom I serve. I rarely have any other women on the leadership teams on which I serve. Because I'm fifty-eight and have been doing this for years, I feel that I'm appreciated and have a voice in what happens on those teams. I have even led some of the teams and have gotten along quite well with the men.

Because of this common respect and close connection with married men (rarely is there a single man on these teams), I am aware that I am a part of the world of these men that often their wives are not privy to. I work closely with them often about challenging issues (both positive and negative), and sometimes their wives are not in the circle of confidentiality.

Therefore, I have always done my very best to build relationships with the wives. I'm intentional about getting to know them and involve them in my relationship with their husbands so that it is a joint relationship. I make sure that outside of my "business time" with their husbands, I communicate with them and, when appropriate, let them know what's going on in the meetings. Husbands often don't give details when communicating with their wives after meetings, even if it is appropriate. At times this communication comes via email or other media due to geographical distances.

When I have sensed a wife is insecure about my relationship with her husband, I have made sure to "step back" and be more businesslike for a time. I have learned that this is usually a personal issue for that wife, and not necessarily me. This took some time for me to understand, and I have learned not to project her emotions on to me.

Also, when speaking to the men with whom I serve, I always speak of their wives and ask them to give my greetings to them.

In building healthy, sacred, sibling-style relationships with the opposite sex, we don't do so naively. We need to be self-aware and in touch with our emotions. We pray and ask the Holy Spirit to keep us sensitive to his leading, with the glory of Jesus as our highest motivation. I find that when I am tempted to "hide" something from my spouse, this is a warning to me that I should tread softly. This goes for anything, not just relationships!

Some couples have separated or divorced as a result of increased access to past relationships via social media. When tempted to look up an old flame online, be on your guard! Beware of the needs that arise from the overwhelming loneliness and fatigue that occur after huge successes. We must know ourselves. Beyond that, we need friends who ask us tough questions—friends who truly know us and hold us accountable. This helps us to build honorable relationships.

God intervened in one couple's relationship when the wife recognized she was having an "emotional affair" with a coworker. Confessing and receiving needed help kept the couple together and in ministry.

One single woman shared her experience with emotional attraction and how she dealt with it:

Even though I have done all that I can to prevent the wives of the men with whom I serve [from being] uncomfortable, many years ago I didn't protect my own heart. I was meeting regularly with a group of three men working on a ministry project. I truly enjoyed working with each of the men, but with one of them I was more "connected" in vision, passion, philosophy of ministry, and personality.

During our meetings, I sensed that both of us were connecting in a deeper way than the others. I found that I was looking forward to the meetings because I knew I would be hearing his vision and passion and that we would agree on ministry ideas. I realized somewhere down the road that he too was greatly enjoying our time together. We never spent time alone, yet I found myself becoming emotionally attached to him. I never asked him if he felt the same way, but I believe he did as well.

The Lord convicted me, and I spoke to a dear friend/mentor and asked to be accountable for my thoughts and actions.
I also found a way to no longer be on that ministry team and to step away from any connection with him other than when we were together with his wife present.

A couple of years later his wife came to me and said that she had noticed something going on between her husband and me. She was sure it had not been physical, but she was afraid that she had lost his emotions. She also noticed that I had pulled away from ministry with him. I admitted what had happened in my heart/mind and what I had done once I realized that I was on a downward road. She and I cried together and thanked the Lord that he had protected all three of us from the enemy's attack. She has never told me if she has spoken to him about this situation, and I haven't asked.

We became very close friends, but I still keep a healthy distance from her husband, knowing the past and wanting to be pure. She and I have been accountable to each other for several things over the years due to this very intimate victory over the enemy. I'm thankful for her friendship and for the Lord's protection.

Building sacred-sibling relationships has challenges, but we should not let the possible obstacles keep us from following through on loving one another well and modeling Christlike love to the communities in which we serve. Both married and single people can work together, as well as separately, to build strong, sacred connections.

Family

Marital jealousy and fear of possible moral failure aren't the only issues that may cause singles to feel alienated from married people on teams. There is also the issue of feeling like a perceived threat to family time. Having had four children, I understand the need for family time. I am thankful for the time we invested in our children. I love our kids. I was happy to spend time together, and we guarded days off and time with one another. But we also loved our team and invited them to our home. We did things together.

We served together. We worked through disagreements together, cried together, and rejoiced together. I wanted our kids to know their team aunts, uncles, and cousins. We were in life together. We looked out for each other.

Being balanced in loving our team and loving our family is needed. We cannot idolize our children and make them our entire focused ministry.

A Bible story that haunts me is found in 1 Samuel 2, when "a man of God" comes to confront the high priest Eli for letting his sons persist in evil behavior—taking what should have been dedicated to the Lord for themselves. Through his prophetic messenger, God asks Eli, "Why do you honor your sons more than me?" (1 Sam 2:29).

May this never be true of us! We discipline our children and want them (and us) to honor God. We don't want to be like Eli, ignoring our children as they continue in sin. Nor do we want to be like Eli's sons, taking what is dedicated to the Lord (our children) and keeping them for ourselves! Raising our children is part of what God calls parents to do, but not all that we do.

When we look at the New Testament, we see that raising children is important and parents are exhorted to love and discipline them. But Scripture also points out that our children are not to be the sole focus of our lives. We are God's children as well as parents, called to serve him in the church, our communities, and world. We can see this in Paul's letter to Timothy, where he lists requirements for widows to receive support from the church:

> No widow may be put on the list of widows unless she is over sixty, has been faithful to her husband, and is well known for her good deeds, such as bringing up children, showing hospitality, washing the feet of the Lord's people, helping those in trouble and devoting herself to all kinds of good deeds. (1 Tim 5:9–10)

Women are involved in a broad range of ministries, both inside and outside of their homes. We devote time and energy to ministering to our children, and when they are young this takes a huge portion of our time. But we can always be looking for ways to serve others. This can happen in our homes and maybe less so outside our homes. As our kids get older, we still need to raise and disciple them, but we will have more time in the community.

Children are a large part of a mother and father's work, but we cannot make them our entire world. They are an important part of our world, and nothing brings out the assertive part of me like protecting my kids, even now that they are all in their thirties! If we focus so much on our physical family, however, we may miss possible ministry opportunities in our community. If we neglect time and ministry with our teammates, it is to our detriment and a tremendous loss for our children.

Women talk about balancing ministry roles a lot. However, men conduct ministry in and out of the home also. Making ministry to family a priority, as well as ministering to team and community, is a tall order. It is not impossible, but it takes strategic thinking and intentional planning. It won't just happen.

How are husbands ministering to their wives and children? What are husbands doing to help their families minister to others? I remember our husbands caring for our kids so that my teammate and I could pursue a ministry opportunity.

What are teams doing now to help each other? When single and married teammates plan outreach events, both single and married people attend. How are we encouraging each other in community outreach? How are we building spiritual family ties in our teams that can overflow into communities?

One of my favorite memories is watching my daughter Kristi open a card sent to her for her high school graduation. It was from a former teammate, her "aunt" Marsha. In it was a check and a photo, taken years before, of Marsha holding Kristi. Kristi squealed, "It's from Aunt Marsha!" as the check fell to the ground and she focused on the picture! Of course, she eventually cashed the check! But it was the relationship that mattered, the memories of being loved by our sister in Christ. Our kids were all influenced by loving and godly aunts and uncles, not related by blood but by the Spirit.

Brothers and Sisters

These non-blood family members on our teams involve more than aunts and uncles. We also are brothers and sisters. But it is obvious from the survey that more men than women said that female teammates were seen as sisters in Christ. What were the men doing that was not picked up on, and what weren't they doing that would communicate this?

Suzy remembers a discussion with a team leader who was asking for help in dealing with singles. His team had gone through a painful situation with a single woman, and the whole team was still reeling from the upheaval and wounds. "Can you help us learn how to better deal with singles?" he asked.

> I'm always a bit sensitive to the idea that people need to be "dealt" with in the body of Christ. But I know my coworkers were sincere in asking for help. I shared with this leader that working with singles isn't rocket science. How we treat one another is a gospel issue, and I urged him to think about how he would want his mother, sister, or daughter (he had four of them) to be treated if she served on a team. It was like a lightbulb turned on when he thought of his loved ones. He thanked me for helping him to see it.

> Another question to consider is "Would you be able to look her
> dad or brothers in the eye if they came to visit you?"

In developing sacred-sibling relationships, what do holy brother/sister relationships look like? I did not grow up having brothers. I have one sister. But I've seen my two sons in their roles as older brothers to my daughters. When they were little, they could be a bit rough in how they treated each other! But as they grew older, I saw how they looked out for their sisters. One of my sons took his sister out for breakfast to talk about her future plans. The other son ran almost a mile and a half from our home to a shopping mall to help his sister who was having car troubles. When a young man was interested in dating our daughter, we asked our sons what they thought about him. They gave him their hearty approval.

As adults, they visit each other even when living on different continents. They help each other, and they love each other's kids. They pray for each other. I have no doubts that if one of my daughters needed something from either of their brothers, he would be there for her.

Suzy has brothers, and sisters too. She shares what brotherly love looks like:

> Growing up, my oldest brother always had my back. I knew if I got
> into trouble he'd be there for me. To this day I know I can call on
> him day or night. He called me when his first child was born, and
> again years later to announce he would become a grandfather.
> He finds a way to include me in special times when possible.
>
> My younger brothers are there for me too. I remember a 4:00
> a.m. call after the terrorist attacks in France from one of my
> brothers who had been in the special forces. He wanted to make
> sure I understood the threat these new cells posed and that it
> could be dangerous for me, a soft target, for a long time. He gave
> me all sorts of advice on keeping my head down. I later passed
> on some of his concerns to my teammates, as they went beyond
> the protocols our mission had in place.

We picture sacred-sibling relationships like this: helping, being there, honoring, loving. Certainly there are culturally appropriate ways to do this. But sometimes we may need to act counter to culture to honor women as our sisters.

When asked how they have helped their spiritual sisters, one man responded about the need to have healthy relationships with the opposite sex and still help out other men as well:

Even though I am married, it's important to be able to have healthy and open relationships with members of the opposite sex who are single. It normalizes the relationship and challenges the notion that the only kinds of relationships that one can have with the opposite sex are romantic and sexual. Another thought I had was how single males are often left out of the help and care conversation. Single females, being seen as the "weaker sex," are afforded more help and support, while single males are expected to "man up" and take care of themselves. This isn't true, and the double standard can often be hurtful.

Here are other ways men sought to be a help to their sisters that reflect a sacred-sibling relationship:

"I've been a sounding board and advisor on more and more issues as they moved up into greater areas of responsibility, helping them with my network of contacts and giving them suggestions from my perspective."

"Being part of a conversation with a single gal ([along]with my wife) as she opened up about her abusive father and being a 'safe' male who could give her healthy and positive reinforcement."

"Inviting them over for a meal and simply being a male who sits and listens and converses and gives them a male perspective. Having a movie night every Friday night where our house became a nest of singles (almost all female), and I'd like to think I provided a perspective or presence or something that made it different than *just* a group of single ladies meeting in one another's home. At least they sure enjoyed it, so something was working."

Physical Touch, Spiritual Connection

Physical touch between sexes is always tricky in the missions world. You not only have the culture you grew up in, but different personalities and the host cultures to which you have adapted! What is acceptable in these contexts can range from no touching ever to bear hugs, side hugs, distant hugs with arms extended to avoid further touching, kisses on both cheeks, shaking hands, kissing hands, bowing … all seeking to show friendship—but in so many different ways and trying to be appropriate in each of them!

Some single women can go months without one touch. A woman who had a father and brothers who hugged her goes from constant displays of affection to zero. Other people on our teams may have suffered physical abuse and don't want to be touched by others at all!

How can we show fondness for one another as men and women? Does every touch have to have a sexual connotation? Of course not. Does our teammate want to be touched? As teams, we must talk about touch and what is needed, wanted, or expected as sacred siblings.

One survey respondent suggested ways to build this type of family atmosphere that would be open to discussing needs:

> Be in community together through mixed groups. Men, whether single or married: Let women know they are safe with you, that you're there for them in a protective way, and nothing more, should they need help (anything from a home repair to a ride to the airport when it's late). Women: Step up to invite people over. Have friendships that aren't flirtatious. Be hospitable to everyone.

In societies where women are vulnerable and deemed unvalued, what would it look like when believing men treat them as sacred siblings? When strangers give leering looks, their brothers stand up for them. When snide comments or dirty jokes are made at a woman's expense, their brothers don't laugh—these men confront the sin. When help is needed, as brothers they make sure their sisters get the help they need.

Men's wives must be committed to their sisters, as well, and not selfish with their husband's time and help. How can women be a help to one another? Women are responsible to remember the truth and not allow themselves to be swayed by cultural lies. They know their value in Christ; and no matter what the world throws at them, they recognize they are treasured children of God.

Protecting the Vulnerable

Because of the fallenness of our world ruled by sin, organizations need to develop policies to protect the vulnerable. It is sad, as we should be doing this without needing policy to dictate it, but women and children are often the most vulnerable and need to be protected. Many organizations have developed policies so that those who are vulnerable know any offense or harassment they may experience will be taken seriously and will be addressed. In the policy, procedures are laid out for how to report the abuse and what steps are to be taken next.

How is your organization protecting over half of its members? What is leadership doing to listen to their struggles?

At times, leadership misses an opportunity to be a brother to a sister who is in need. A single woman shared her experience with facing abuse in her organization and feeling powerless because there was no one to stand with her.

> I was once in a very difficult situation, under a boss who was also a part of our organization. I had a separate leader, but the dynamics were a bit awkward. He was new and a bit intimidated by this other guy. Basically, my boss was not in a good place emotionally. He became extremely fearful, controlling, [and] threatening and suddenly decided to change our contract in the middle of the term. It was a huge mess. I had to get various leaders involved. Because I was single, though, I ended up being powerless. I had no one to stand up and say no to this man. The next person in charge was good friends with him and just couldn't see the power dynamics at play.
>
> I ended up being told that I could sign the new agreement or else leave the country. And, in the end, I had to leave. And actually … as a result of this one guy and his wife … there were several ladies who had to leave. The dynamics were extremely abusive, but nobody would listen to us. It seemed that single women didn't matter—at least not enough to make it worth rocking the boat, making anyone upset. It seemed that nobody in leadership had it in mind that abuse could be a real problem. Excuses such as "personality issues," "cultural differences," etc., were used, and the real issues were not addressed.

Abuse and powerlessness are more severe issues. But awkwardness between men and women working together can also be a hurdle.

Caring for One Another

I was once the only woman on a committee working on a project. It was great in that, for the first time ever, I didn't have to wait in a line at the women's restroom! The meetings were productive. My voice was valued, and the men wanted to hear my insights and opinions. I wanted to hear theirs. Discussions went well and relationships were developing. Until the group photo. The men huddled together. I must not have been huddleable. One man said he wanted to stand by this other man, and I kind of shuffled to the side. I felt—well, *unwanted* is too strong of a word, because I had felt wanted all week! I felt like all of a sudden I was on the sidelines and nobody knew quite what to do with me.

Please keep in mind, this is all my perception of what was happening. I didn't think anyone else noticed until another person, who was also a minority, pulled me into the picture. All was then right in my world. He took the initiative as my brother in Christ to make me feel valued and a part of the group.

Everyone in the world should have the opportunity to be a minority so that we develop empathy for one another. My brother saw my need, and as a sacred sibling he sought to meet it.

Suzy sharess a story where helping a sister almost didn't happen.

> A single friend was working on a film project in a faraway place. She was staying in a guesthouse in a dicey part of town, about a mile from the missionaries she was filming. One night after dinner it was already dark, and she needed to get home. She found herself up against the Billy Graham principle. The couple had always had an agreement that he would never ride with another woman on his motorcycle. But this meant there was no way for my friend to get home safely. There were three options. 1) Let the "brother" give her a lift anyway. 2) Let his wife take her, but that put the wife at risk, coming home alone in the same dangerous neighborhood. 3) Let their single sister go alone and hope for the best.

> My single friend shared with me how awkward it was to hear the couple have a huge fight over whether to help her or not! I think they eventually agreed that he could drive her home, due to the dangers she could face, but it was tense for all of them. It put them all in a tricky situation—and she'd come to serve and help them with this project.

How to care for one another isn't always clear, especially in cultures that are not our own. But I wonder if we make it more difficult than it needs to be. When we think "Our sister needs a ride," it becomes clearer that we must help her. How to do so can be figured out.

In communities that have not been transformed by the power of God, there is no clue how to have healthy, godly brother/sister relationships, as this is only possible in the body of Christ. Even where the church is strong, these sibling relationships are not as strong as they could be or should be. Our teams have the opportunity to model the family of God in culturally appropriate ways, as well as positively clashing with societal norms, when they demonstrate a sacred-sibling mind-set.

In much of this chapter we have talked about the responsibility of men to be brothers to their sisters. We'd like to also urge women to think about how they treat their brothers in Christ. Do we seek opportunities to affirm and encourage them regularly? It is often easier to point out when others hurt us. Do we tell them when they do things right? Do we applaud them and cheer for them? What do we do that makes it hard to treat us as sisters?

Can we be forgiving when they mess up? Bitterness is an epidemic throughout the missionary world. These are things that must be discussed as teams. Men, let us know what you need from your sisters. How can we come alongside you in ways that honor you? How can we love you better?

Relationships are never a one-way street. Let's covenant to work together as sacred siblings. Surely as ones who have experienced the greatest love, forgiveness, and grace of God, we can in turn offer love, practice forgiveness, and extend grace as sacred siblings.

When we are loved well within our spiritual family, contentment in our marital status should have easier soil in which to flourish. Contentment is always a possible choice, even when circumstances are uncomfortable. But as sacred siblings, we do all we can to help each other choose it! Our next chapter looks at contentment.

Good Ideas and Helpful Tools

A helpful resource for married couples is available on ChristianityToday.com: "It's Not Billy Graham Rule or Bust (15 ways my husband and I guard our marriage while still loving our friends of the opposite sex)," by Tish Harrison Warren. Read this article and discuss as a team or region. Warren mentions how she and her husband not only protect their marriage but build into it. Communication between them is key.

Edwards (2008, 191) quotes an email from John Ortberg in which he uses three tests in building fences that protect his marriage but allow for building friendships with his sisters. These obviously can be used by women, as well, in building friendships with brothers.

- **FIRST,** the *Sibling Test*—He asks, "Do I trust this woman as I would my sister?" Ortberg knows that you can't trust every woman. There are some needy, emotionally immature women who need Jesus, and men need to be discerning enough to entrust their care to seasoned female staff members.

- **SECOND,** the *Screen Test*—He asks, "Would I be embarrassed if any of our conversations or actions were on a movie screen?"

- **THIRD,** the *Secret Test*—"Am I keeping anything secret from my wife?"

From the book *Single Mission,* here are twelve positive steps for helping singles—actually everyone—maintain sexual purity:
- Maintain a vibrant spiritual life.
- Acknowledge your feelings and thoughts, and bring them to God.
- Build friendships.
- When struggling, contact a friend.
- Tackle stress, and take exercise.
- Find healthy ways to meet your needs.
- Reduce risk.
- Value intimacy more than sex.
- Have a hug.
- Enjoy other pleasures in life.
- Seek help from others, have an accountability partner, and remember this is a battle for nearly everyone.
- Receive forgiveness if you sin. (Hawker and Herbert 2013, 116–20)

Application Question

- How could modeling sacred-sibling relationships affect your community?

CHAPTER 11

The Secret of Being Content Can Be Learned

STATEMENT

I am content in my current marital status.

MEAN
Married 3.81
Single 3.08

P-VALUE
.000

MEAN
Female 3.37
Male 3.74

P-VALUE
.000

The research is not saying that *all* married people are content in their marriages and *all* single people are discontent in their singleness. Nor is it saying that all men are content in their marital status and all women are not. It is pointing to a significant difference in the sense of contentment regarding marital status between those who are married and those who are not, as well as between genders. More married cross-cultural workers are content with their current marital status than those who are single. More men are content in their current marital status than women are. A large majority of those men are married.

Contentedness is a tricky thing. As soon as we think we have it, it can disappear! In his letter to the Philippians, Paul wrote about learning to be content in regard to being in need and having an abundance.

> I am not saying this because I am in need, for I have learned to be content whatever the circumstances. I know what it is to be in need, and I know what it is to have plenty. I have learned the secret of being content in any and every situation, whether well fed or hungry, whether living in plenty or in want. I can do all this through him who gives me strength. (Phil 4:11–13)

Paul states that contentment is learned and the way to be content isn't obvious. There is a secret that can be learned to being content in all circumstances! Of course, he points to Christ who empowers us.

In a presentation at a Shoulder to Shoulder conference, Barry Danylak pointed out that living with unfulfilled desire is normal for everyone. We all have something that we want and don't have. Some of these things seem major, and some are minor. It is how we live with the unfulfilled desires that determines our contentedness in Christ.

When Christ isn't our focus, it is much, much easier to lose a sense of contentment. When we spend a lot of time on Facebook, for instance, we find that the secret to being content is not found there. Facebook is more about staging life than real life. The marriage proposals, baby-gender reveals, exotic vacations, color-coordinated family photos … Facebook is a place where we can choose what we share, and we usually share only the positive images. If we think a photo makes us look fat, we don't post that one. If we look thin, we are more likely to share that one! It is easy to portray the best of life—that brief five-second pose after hours of preparation—and people may think that the picture we choose is normal. It isn't.

Spending too much time on social media is making contentment more elusive than it has to be. When you're single and longing to be married, seeing all the posts of your friends' fairy-tale engagements and pristine weddings makes it easy to long even more for that. But on Facebook you don't see the newlyweds' first fight, the ugly silence, the difficulties in communication that make both of them feel like giving up. Only the pretty pictures are portrayed. And if we're married, it's easy to see single people's world travels and adventurous lives, but we don't see the lonely nights or the grief of being childless.

Facebook has been called Fakebook, and to an extent we need to be careful how much we buy into what we are viewing and determine if it is having an effect on our contentment.

We tend to compare ourselves with others anyway. When our focus is on each other instead of Christ, we ask the wrong questions. Whose spiritual gift is more important? Who is serving in the most difficult places? What is our position or level of leadership, and how does it compare with where someone else is?

For those who are married and long for the single life, we see the ease of travel, the adventures with friends, the spur-of-the-moment activities; and we long for that, as we are restricted by another person's schedule and vacation preferences. When kids are small and we can't even go to the bathroom alone, the alone time is enviable enough without adding all of the picture-perfect outings for coffee with friends or fun hobbies.

I (Sue) enjoy watching old reruns of *I Love Lucy*. Seeing the friendship between Lucy and Ethel has always produced a longing in my heart for one best friend. I have wanted an Ethel for my Lucy life. I have many friends and lots of acquaintances, but there is no Ethel in my life. I think single people have an advantage in that they are more able to have deep, lasting, best-friend relationships. Don doesn't want to be my Ethel, nor should he be. He is my Ricky! It could be that this isn't an issue related to marital status; maybe it is due to the many times we've moved or to my personality.

I asked Suzy, "Do you have an Ethel? Do more singles you know have these deep friendships?" Although Suzy knows both marrieds and singles who struggle with loneliness and don't have lots of deep friendships, here is how she answered:

> Actually, I have several Ethels and a few Fred and Ethels (and some Lucys and Rickys too)! I have especially needed close friends and mentors in my life who help me keep things in perspective. The grass will always be greener in other places if we don't take care of our own lawn. Just as married couples must work hard to keep their marriage healthy and God-honoring, singles need to work hard to keep their singleness healthy and God-honoring. Singles tend to imagine deep intimacy and companionship and shared burdens as the norm for couples in ministry. We don't think of all the hard stuff any more than married people did before they got married.
>
> If sexual intimacy is one of the blessings of marriage, freedom is a blessing of singleness. It's funny how both sides want what they can't have. Paul warned about this trade-off in 1 Corinthians 7. It's sad that our mission agencies and churches rarely talk about this. I've always felt that the "caught" message, if not the "taught" one, is that you can have it all if you're married and that singleness is somehow a lesser calling. As singles, we are free to dictate our schedules and serve wholeheartedly and without distraction. But there are some hard things too, many of which have already been mentioned.
>
> In the end, we were all created for deep relationship, and the Bible never intended that our singleness be lived in isolation. And marriage wasn't intended to be the only answer to relationship needs either. I think men and women all need good spiritual friendships to help us in this adventure called life. That's where our sacred siblings come in.

Married and single people tend to want the best of each other's worlds without recognizing the challenges that "best" entails! The grass is not always greener on the other side of the fence. Each side has green grass and troublesome weeds!

There is also an ebb and flow of contentment in different aspects of our lives. One team member said, "Don't compare the best side of being single with the worst side of being married, and vice versa."

For a married person with children, life with young children is extremely busy, and contentment could come and go with the next crisis—a forgotten birthday or anniversary, potty training, schooling decisions, culture stress, ministry failures, and plain sinfulness.

For a single person, contentment might be challenged by the next big birthday. The biological clock is ticking for women, and as the hope of having children diminishes a bit with every passing year, they may feel more desperate about marriage. It has been said that between thirty and forty years of age there is more pressure; before that and after that, it is not as great.

We have already mentioned having spiritual children. Bethany Jenkins (2016) wrote about her experience of being a part of a spiritual family and the comfort it gave her in the midst of childlessness.

> I also think "family" is more than formal adoptive relationships. As a Christian, I find comfort and security in the knowledge I am part of a spiritual family. When someone trusts in Christ, she becomes a member of the household of faith as an adopted child of God. Other Christians become her brothers and sisters, and she is to love them in deeply significant ways.

Oh that the church would put spiritual motherhood and fatherhood back in a place of honor! What grand teachable moments Mother's Day and Father's Day could become.

Childlessness is also an issue in regard to contentment for some couples, as well as singles. When the desire to have children isn't becoming a reality, life is grievous and faith-challenging. Thinking through adoption, or medical solutions, or acceptance of "It is what it is" is difficult. The desire is strong!

A comforting and encouraging resource when faced with the disappointment and grief of childlessness is Danylak's "A Biblical-Theological Perspective on Singleness." He emphasizes the joys of producing spiritual children:

> Beyond the theological significance of this passage [Isaiah 54] stands a message of great comfort to those who are single or childless within the church. For like the barren woman, despite the absence of physical children, they too can rejoice in the prospect of "bearing" spiritual children, whom they will raise and nurture in the good news of the gospel message. This shift is a message of great joy to those unable to experience the joy of having physical

children. For in the paradigm of the new covenant, the people of God are no longer defined through physical birth but through spiritual re-birth. Those unable to experience the joy of physical children are still able to experience profound joy and satisfaction in producing spiritual children through evangelism and service to the kingdom. (2006, 12)

Getting married and having children are normal desires for almost all humans. They are good desires. At one point, Suzy was ashamed of her desire for marriage, so she never admitted it to others. She writes:

God began to show me that longing for intimacy was really something he had put in all human hearts and that, at its core, it was a longing for him! That really freed me to embrace the ache and to go deeper with God and others about it. I learned that there is a tension and a great difference between acknowledging pain or struggle, or even disappointment, and whining, demanding, or throwing a pity party. Jim Elliot's famous words, "Don't let your longings take the place of your living," were a great exhortation to me. It was the recipe to keeping my heart soft and in touch with God, as opposed to becoming bitter or living in denial.

This journey was also an excellent place to test God's goodness and sufficiency at each turn. I came to see that he really is enough. It didn't numb or remove the longings, but it nudged me toward the one who could be trusted to hold them, and to satisfy them in ways I'd never envisioned.

From what we hear, churches and some mission agencies strongly encourage men to get married before they go overseas. They might encourage women to get married also, but it seems to be more socially acceptable for women to go as singles. However, some churches might not want to take on single women's support because they consider it a strong possibility that single women won't end up serving long-term. They may meet a man and get married, leaving the mission field.

If those in leadership do not consider singleness a viable option for long-term ministry, we will lose valuable teammates. When those who are married keep trying to find a mate for their single coworkers or tease them about finding Mr. or Mrs. Right, there will be stress. Married teammates must listen to their single teammates, as they may need to verbally process how they are doing in learning contentment as single believers. Single people must listen to their married teammates, as they may also need to process some of their challenges as husbands and wives.

For those who are single, if your discontentment blinds you to the challenges of marriage, be aware that there are married people who are also discontent! Discontent is equally available to all!

Each person is responsible for his or her choices regarding contentment. However, a question we need to also ask ourselves is "How does the church, our culture, and our mission's view of family feed into reasons for making discontentment in our marital status easier to choose?" Are we affirming the role of singles in the body of Christ? Have we idealized family to the extent that, as one survey respondent put it, "We have demonized singleness"? As brothers and sisters in Christ, we need to evaluate where our wrong messages or lack of affirmation may be increasing the struggles of our coworkers.

One survey respondent shared about contentment in singleness and the influence of host cultures:

> I think our host culture accepts singleness better than some host cultures, thus the view of singleness on teams is better. (Most of the teams I have been on reflect my host culture.) However, I do know ladies [who] think everyone should be married, which sometimes, I think, can be hard on the single ladies [who] are working hard to be content with the situation that the Lord has put them in.

All of us who have thought, at one time or another, "This isn't how I thought life would be," need people to love us and point us to the truth that this is how life is and we must trust the God who sovereignly put us here. Community can do that for us, so our next chapter looks at that.

Good Ideas and Helpful Tools

Singles should not feel pressured or encouraged to get married or be discouraged from contentment in singleness (1 Corinthians 7). Don't seek to change people's marital status. Rather, walk with them to be content in whatever season they are in today. Single people have value apart from being in relationships or producing children in a marriage.

Joshua Becker in his article, "The Unmistakable Freedom of Contentment and How to Find It," mentions six ways to learn contentment:

1. Become grateful.

2. Take control of your attitude.

3. Break the habit of satisfying discontentment with acquisitions.

4. Stop comparing yourself to others.

5. Help others.

6. Be content with what you have, never with what you are.

Application Question

- How does contentment, or the lack of it, influence team relationships?

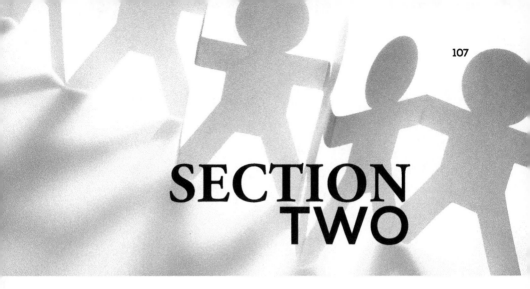

SECTION TWO

Issues Revealed From a Single's Perspective

As we examined the statements with which singles agreed more than married people, we noticed that they all had to do with expectations: what singles were expecting from their teams and what their teams or organizations were expecting from them.

We will look at expectations in regard to community, being seen as mature, receiving practical help from teammates, and ministry involvement—focusing particularly on the different perspectives married and single people shared.

Explore these four areas with us, none of which have easy answers but all of which will provide good discussion points for teams.

CHAPTER 12

Expecting Community and Finding Loneliness

STATEMENT	MEAN
I thought my team would be like a family, but it does not provide the community I need.	Married 1.71 Single 1.93 P-VALUE .050

More single people than married people expected their team to be like a family. The key word here is *expected*. It looks like more single individuals than married individuals expected stronger community from their teams. Also, it appears that what they experienced on their teams did not match their expectations of what team should be—resulting, consequently, in disappointment.

From a married person's perspective, I (Sue) don't think I was looking for family in my team, probably because I was coming with my own small family. I didn't really know what to expect from a team—possibly good friends and coworkers. We began our first term of service with a single woman. The three of us met together weekly as a team for prayer, support, and encouragement. Soon others joined us, and we continued our weekly meetings. We also did fun things together; we often had the meetings in our home because of our children. We enjoyed some activities together.

Because we were in a conservative Muslim culture, Don and I, as a married couple, felt like we were seen as the protectors of our single teammates. We took on the role of older siblings according to that culture. When singles were interested in dating each other, they often did so in our home. It wasn't the most romantic place, with four children running around, but it was a safe place.

As team leaders, and also as the "older siblings," Don and I took our family responsibility seriously. We protected our single women from unwanted marriage proposals, as much as we could, by being the "gatekeepers." If we had a single female teammate in our home when an unbelieving single man from our host country was coming to visit, she would go out the side door while the man entered through the front. She didn't need more marriage proposals from unbelievers! Due to the pressures our sisters were experiencing, we felt the need to protect them quite keenly.

Because each person's needs and values differ, it can be tricky to know how intentional one should be about becoming family. When we lovingly confront members of our team, does it come only from the heart of a leader or can they also feel the heart of a sacred sibling? One single woman on our team began developing a relationship with another expat worker in the community. Because Don and I saw some red flags, we talked with her. We talked with her as leaders, but also because we loved her as our sister in Christ. It was a necessary but difficult time for all of us! I thank God for her trusting but breaking heart in following through on our suggestion to end the dating relationship.

In another situation, because we were seen as a single man's "parents" (although he was older than us, we were seen as his leaders and family away from family), we represented him to the father of the woman he wanted to marry. She was older than us too! But it was part of our commitment to be family to one another on our team and to lead our small community well.

We must remember, though, that not all singles and not all marrieds want the same thing from their team. This is why it is so important to make this a talking point for people before they arrive and as they join the team. What does the team look like? How do we function? How much time do we spend together? Taking the time to understand potentially differing opinions and expectations is essential to a healthy team.

In order to understand varying perspectives, let's look at some differing points of view from some of our single respondents.

There are those who wanted their team to be like family.

> "I know that as a single there is more of a desire for community and family; since married couples already have that (and have other obligations), it is often difficult for them to provide this as well. What would help is if there were more explicit exploration of how this could be worked out—including, perhaps, trading services and making sacrifices."

> "A bigger deal is made about a family arriving or returning, rather than a person. But I would suggest that the single person needs the welcome even more than the family, precisely because they're coming by themselves and have a greater need to feel connected."

Some felt very strongly about wanting to develop deeper relationships on the team, but sometimes felt excluded by their team because the nuclear family had no time or desire to include them.

"I don't think that my being single impacts their decisions about spending time with me; I just think they have a lot going on and either can't or simply aren't actually interested in taking time for us to cultivate our relationship. I mean, in the message I wrote on Saturday I gave my entire week's schedule to know when we could have a good chat and coffee, because she asked, and I haven't heard back. I know that things come up as a married person with children, but it gets to a point, as a single person, that you just feel unwanted and not cared about, and that can be painful."

"Being single, I tend to be the one [who] goes to them to spend time with [teammates] and the one [who] usually calls and reaches out. I understand, but it can be exhausting."

There were also single people who expressed that they weren't looking for family in their teams and thought that this wasn't a productive way to view team.

"The singles cannot depend only on the couples/families for their sense of community."

"The question about team as a family ... just want to comment that I don't believe everyone wants that. Also, I feel that people on teams should generally not seek to get most of their needs met via the team.... I think it is healthy to have a mix of outside relationships and relationships on the team."

Singles do not have a built-in support person, such as is normally found in a spouse. If the team isn't there for them when they are struggling to hang on, especially in the beginning, they may not stay. If teams can face things together and be a support system for each other, even if not quite like a family, we can be an encouragement to one another.

Mission organizations need to be intentional in pre-field training as they teach about teams. If the presenter has been on a "family-type" team, her material may have a bias toward that dynamic as she presents examples of team life. If a particular theory of team is presented, but that ideal isn't found on the field, newcomers are set up for disappointment!

How can we help people prepare for what is ahead? It would be profitable for newcomers to communicate with their future teammates early in the process to clarify what each is expecting and what is reality.

Finding community inside and outside of the team is important for single people. Suzy shares her own example:

Over time, French believers have become my community. My holidays are now with them more than with my team. We are all created for community and need community, and this is why it matters. I think it's especially important when we first arrive in a new culture or ministry. And singles may feel the need for community even more strongly, as we leave our families behind when we follow God's call.

My first holidays tended to be spent with my teammates. As relationships were formed and grew stronger, my community grew to include a whole new spiritual family of French people. It's been a long time since I spent any holidays with teammates, but only because my French friends invite me into their homes around the special dates. Or I invite French people into my home on certain holidays. I've also seen that this is one of the lovely opportunities singles have to bond even more deeply in cultures. Families and friends adopt us in ways that they don't adopt my "married-with-children" teammates.

I think we would all agree that no one wants to be overly dependent on the team. We cannot expect everything to come from them, but we do recognize we need each other's support. I don't think I would have lasted our first term without the support of teammates. We want good, healthy relationships. We want to explore what that looks like for each member of our team.

Families need to be inclusive with singles, but not to the detriment of their own family time. How couples balance their family time and include single workers into their lives will differ from team to team. But it must be done—even if we don't necessarily view our team as family or want that label.

We must have good relationships that model the loving one another and caring for one another that is taught and was practiced in the New Testament. One of my favorite passages of Scripture is Romans 16, where Paul mentions his many coworkers and his love and appreciation for them—some of whom were married and some of whom were single.

At times I am worried that families so protect their family time that physical family has become an idol. This results in sacrificing the eternal spiritual family of God for family that is temporal. I thank God that Don and I invested in our family time and in our children. I thank God that we also invested in spiritual family and that our children saw these relationships modeled. Did we balance things perfectly? No, of course not. But we endeavored to honor commitments to both family systems.

Singles need to invite families in as well, but not to the detriment of their own outside friendships and to the exclusion of forming other relationships.

I would say, as a married person, that it is also important for those who are married to build relationships outside of team (and outside of family). I have experienced both a team that was my most important support network and a team in which I had to find that support elsewhere. The transition from one to the other was painful because of the expectation that things on the new team should be as they had been on our previous team. It was like going from a basketball team to a relay team: all working together for one goal to all working together but in different directions towards different goals.

Regarding family, it is also wise to build friendships outside of our homes. I remember going to an aerobics center, not because I love to exercise but because I wanted to build friendships outside of who I was and what I did at home. It made for a healthier me at home and gave me opportunities to influence those in my community and to be influenced by them.

We want to introduce to you an example of not only viewing team as family but living out life as a family: a concept that has been referred to as household-to-household evangelism. This is where single(s) and married people on a team join together to form a household. This household is then able to reach out to other households of extended family in their own host cultures.

As teams intentionally model spiritual family, they can open more doors of ministry into communities. Aidan Till explains what this looks like in an article entitled "Family Plus" (2018, 20–21):

> Mira was reinforcing a point from *The Jesus Storybook Bible* to her boyfriend, Milo, at my dinner table. Mira and Milo were nominal Muslims, raised in the capital of the Central Asian country where we served on a disciple-making team. Mira came to dinner often, sometimes bringing Milo; and each time, they overheard me discipling my four children at our table after dinner.

> As the head of my house and a good host, after reading the stories to my children, I'd carefully explain them to our guests in the local language, since it's rude to talk past someone and not include them. Since Milo spoke better Russian than local, Mira would explain them a second time to him, sharing with him the beauty and goodness of Jesus (whom she hadn't even met), without ever having to navigate the awkward social obligations that would have come with me preaching directly to them over the meal. It was kind of awesome.

This sort of nearly effortless discipleship of a young Muslim couple was only possible because Julie, a single American woman in her thirties, lived with us in our home, as part of our household. Mira was Julie's friend long before she was ours, and it was the freedom that came with Julie's singleness, combined with the testimony of a redeemed family and a Godward head of the house, that provided a context for Mira and Milo to have repeated, rich, textured exposures to the gospel and its effects on multiple generations of people, all at my table.

This goes way back. Jesus did this from Simon Peter's house. Paul did it from Aquila and Priscilla's house. In fact, Paul's entire practical ecclesiology assumes that the church is built with *oikoi* (households). In Paul's time, households included a head, his family, their extended family, employees, the family business, and the physical plant. Think *FamilyPlus.*

For Paul, house churches aren't miniature versions of big-church, just in a house. They're a full house being transformed, activated, and networked to fill communities with Christ. In Colossians Paul unpacks a rich Christology, then teaches us to live Christ out, not in the artificial relationships of programmed Christianity, or even in the too-tight space provided by a nuclear family, but in the more complex relationships of a household. And in 1 Corinthians he says to order our lives, not like Stephanas, but like his household (16:15).

"Okay, fine," you might say. "Singles and families living together might make sense *back then* in Paul's time, or *'over there'* in a foreign culture. But it's not practical here in the West." I vigorously disagree. If it worked back then and it works "over there," it probably works here and now. In fact, it may just offer an alternative story of singleness and of family life that could challenge false assumptions that have crippled the mission and the spiritual formation of the church in the West for generations.

There are obvious benefits. Singles get lonely, maybe more often than married people. Humans are social creatures, designed to live in multi-generational social groups. Because of the profoundly individualistic cultural narrative in the West, we assume lonely people need to get married. But sometimes, people aren't lonely because they need a spouse. They're lonely because they need a family. Some of us are called to be single, but we're not called to be alone, or to exist in some weird limbo between the kids' table and the grownups.' One can be single, be a contributing adult, and not be alone.

Living together in a household requires vulnerability, laying down significant freedom, and purposefully making room. These three practices, it turns out, are deeply resonant with the texture of the gospel. When we open ourselves, embrace limits, and make room every day for each other's gifts and weakness, we model the gospel in ways that let the world *experience* Christ at depths we can't *explain* it to them. Further, those postures can uncouple *us* from pursuits that run deep in our blood and counter to Jesus' dreams for our own hearts—pursuits like clinging to life, misunderstanding liberty, and worshiping happiness.

Practically, living this way can unlock significant resources (time and money) for ministry. Having Julie in our home means that I don't have to decide, after a long day teaching at the university, whether I'm going to go create relationships with seekers or spend time with my children. Julie can cast the line, and the family can land the fish. Sometimes, the single member(s) of a household can forego building their careers for a while to focus all their time and attention on making disciples, while the family with whom they live can play a strong supporting role, providing the context to teach people how to live in God's family. Alternatively, everyone can work *and* minister, expanding the network of people the house can touch, diverting funds that would have gone to two or three house payments into worthy causes.

Sure, not every family is cut out for this, and probably no family is at every stage of life. The same is true for singles. There are ways of being unhealthy in our souls that can be healed living this way, and other kinds of unhealth for which this lifestyle is the wrong prescription. But for most of us, practicing hospitality, vulnerability, and submission to another's needs in this way could re-activate our homes, increasing their reach in the world and diversifying the paths by which the transforming love of Jesus can penetrate the deep places of our hearts.

We can draw new maps for family and singleness if we're willing to experiment a little. I'm convinced it will only take a few households with enough heart and moxie to strike out into waters too long forgotten, and to see how Jesus meets us there.[1]

---

1 This article was originally published in *Revive* magazine. Used with permission.

Good Ideas and Helpful Tools

Best Practices from the Survey:

WHEN I ARRIVED, I told one of the couples that I would like to spend time with their family. We ended up establishing a routine that I had dinner at their house each Sunday evening after church, and I have loved the opportunity to be part of their family and spend time with them. In addition, the husband in this family privately told me that he would be happy to watch their children at any time that I wanted to arrange a time to go out to coffee with his wife. So about once a week the wife and I met and spent a few hours in a cafe. It was a wonderful way for me to develop a closer relationship with her, since I was working with her husband often but saw her much less, and also to give her a chance to get out of the house and away from homeschooling/parenting."

SPEND TIME TOGETHER AND BE INTENTIONAL in fostering relationships. I often tell people that not only do singles need families, but families also need singles. Married people need friendships other than their spouse—singles are often a good source of that friendship. Singles and marrieds need the perspective of life and situations that the other marital status brings—as long as the perspective of one "status" doesn't dominate the relationship. There has to be a mutual give-and-take, as with any other healthy relationship. Celebrate milestones together; be a safe haven for one another."

ANOTHER MALE TEAMMATE and I went over for game night, hosted by a single woman. It was a fun night for everyone, with a lot of joking and teasing. The comment that our host had as we were leaving was that she missed having this kind of big-brother type of camaraderie."

Helpful Tool from a Sister Agency:

One thing team leaders might like to try to build a sense of community for its members is meeting with each team member monthly. The following are some questions written for single women (by single women), but we think these questions would be helpful for any on the team [in order] to foster relationship.

It is suggested that team leader couples (not just the team leader wife or team leader spouse) discuss these next questions with their team member monthly. The only question we believe some ladies may feel uncomfortable talking about with a male team leader is the singleness question. If so, please save that one to talk over with a woman leader!

Catch up

- How are you?

- What's new? Are there any new needs you have that the team should be aware of? How can the team help meet those needs?

- How have you been doing overall in regard to the things mentioned last time we talked?
  What has gone better?
  What still needs to be improved upon or addressed?

Team life

- Do you feel included in the team?
  If not, what would need to change to include you more?

- Do you feel included on God's team?
  If not, what would need to change to include you more?

- How has team life been since these questions were last asked?
  In your opinion, what has gone better?
  In your opinion, what still needs to be improved upon or addressed?

- Are there any areas you think we can grow in as a team?

Language learning

- How is language learning going?

- Is there anything we can do to support you more in this?

Work

- How is it going?

- Is there anything we can do to support you more in this?

Social

- How is it going? How are your relationships with local people?
  With other expats?

- Is there anything we can do to support you more in this?

Living arrangements

- How is it going?

- Is there anything we can do to support you more in this?

Hobbies

- How is it going?
- Is there anything we can do?!

Spiritual health

- How's it going? How are your times with God going? What do you feel God is teaching you right now?
- Is there anything we can do to support you in this?
- How can we facilitate you using your spiritual gifts?

Other gifting/talents/passions

- Are you pursuing your gifts/talents/passions?
- Is there anything we can do to facilitate development of these?

Singleness

- How is God meeting your emotional needs right now?
- How are you doing with being single right now?
- Is there anything else you want us to know?
- Are there any emotional, physical, or spiritual needs that aren't being met right now? What are they and how do you plan to address that? How can we as a team help you do that?

Scheduling

- How is your timetable?
- Do we need to change/update anything?

The following segment was also included to help team leaders.

ADVICE SECTION!

This may not apply to every single person, but it's worth getting to know your team member[s] to see if this applies to them!

- Lots of single women value time with families, with the freedom to sometimes stay for a short time, sometimes a bit longer.

- Lots of single women appreciate having meals with families on occasion.

- Lots of single women enjoy being included on an occasional outing with a family, especially if it requires transportation that she doesn't have access to normally.

- Be aware of giving team updates/reflections, e.g., feedback on what God is doing in your local town to the whole team, including singles!

- Think about offering to help with tasks that may be difficult for your team member to perform alone—e.g., paying bills, buying household items, exploring the locality.

- Things for the team leader couple to let the single person know:

  1. Are there any new singles in the area that the person would be able to connect with through visits, phone calls, and/or email?

  2. Are there any national or international gatherings of singles going on?

Application Questions

- Whether seeking to be like a family or not, how could having good community change your life?
- How could it change the lives of your teammates?

CHAPTER 13

Expecting to Be Considered Mature, but Disappointed

STATEMENT

I am seen as a little sister or little brother on my team who is not treated like an adult.

MEAN
Married 1.10
Single 1.48

P-VALUE
.000

MEAN
Males 1.09
Females 1.40

P-VALUE
.002

It seems as if a common misconception is that there is a strong correlation between marriage and maturity. As a married person who was still sticking my tongue out at my husband behind his back when I was in my forties, I (Sue) can point out that this isn't necessarily true!

As mentioned in an earlier chapter, in many of the cultures where respondents served, single people were not considered mature even if they were older. These cultures would consider marriage as a prerequisite to maturity, no matter how old or mature the single person is. Some youth groups in countries where we served included people in their teens through their thirties. Everyone past childhood who was not married was in the youth group! In some Western churches, as well, single people are often overlooked for leadership roles or ministry opportunities because they aren't considered mature. Perhaps, in some cases, they are immature, but that shouldn't be assumed due to their marital status.

During some family holidays or reunions, those who are single are sometimes still expected to sit at the children's table. This can be quite demoralizing for those who are in their thirties and are working and self-supporting!

Survey respondents shared some of their experiences:

"Those who are not married are often seen as having a junior status."

"Unmarried women, no matter their age, are considered 'girls.'"

"Single men are given less respect."

"Unmarried men are seen as boys in our host culture also, which means married men have different status and opportunities [than] those who are not married."

In some organizations, as well, it seems more married people are considered for leadership roles than those who are single. There is also a significant difference between men and women. Single men do not feel like they are seen as a little brother as much as single women feel like they are seen as a little sister.

This came up in our organization a few years ago when some young single women were serving in a war-torn country. Due to security threats, their leaders asked them to return to their home country for debriefing and discussions on future ministry roles. After the ladies talked with their sending church, mission leadership, and their families, they felt the need to return. One of the complaints they had with leadership was that they treated them as "little sisters" or "daughters" rather than called, capable women. They had already counted the cost, knew what they were facing, and considered Jesus worthy of the risk.

They were asked to get more training in crisis prevention and more fully develop contingency plans. Leaders also apologized and rectified attitudes. It was very humbling, and also inspiring, watching them handle concerns with grace and, at the same time, determination to follow through on God's call.

There were also some men who commented that they didn't think they were viewed as capable because of their single status.

"The single men are perhaps subconsciously expected to minister more to the boys/teenagers, due to the host culture's view of them as youths due to not being married."

"Single men are still seen as 'youth' regardless of age in [the] host culture ... sometimes the same thinking seeps into the team mind-set."

Experience and age are two factors we must consider. One respondent wrote, "I believe that the age of the singles and marrieds is also an important factor. Maturity makes a great difference in how one can handle conflict."

Those who were younger more keenly felt like younger siblings, as did those with less experience. It is natural to assume that with age and experience comes more maturity, so this feeling like a younger sibling would probably diminish after some time. However, we need to examine our perceptions of maturity! Are we expecting more maturity from those who are married than those who are single? Does this lead us to dismiss the ideas and thoughts of our single teammates without hearing them out?

Team members should be sensitive to this and be sure to respect the opinions and ideas of those who are newer and younger. At times, bright ideas and effective suggestions can come from those who arrive and see things from a different perspective. A young, single short-termer came to live and serve in a village in the Middle East. God used him to lead an anti-Jesus man to Christ!

When young people with fresh vision come to teams with older, experienced people, we owe it to our team and to ourselves to listen well! There is no need to feel threatened or judged inadequate; rather we must accept, with open arms, new ideas as possibilities to think and pray about.

Young people joining teams must also be open to listening to those with experience and not just dismiss their ideas out of hand as old-fashioned or narrow-minded. Anticipate what you can learn from people who have been around a while. Do not be arrogant nor overconfident.

The most competent I ever felt was when I was on the plane headed for my first term in cross-cultural ministry. I had been to Bible college, read books, attended classes on evangelism, and led women's Bible studies. I felt prepared and ready to change the world. Had I known that was going to be the last time I felt that competent, I might have savored the moment more!

My vision to change the world was really not so much a vision as it was self-focused unrealistic expectations. I wanted what I did to matter; I wanted my life to be significant, and I thought it would gain significance because of the strengths I was bringing for God to use. Trying to hide, deny, or ignore weaknesses, I wanted people to be impressed with me. It didn't take long to realize that I couldn't hide my weaknesses—they were even more apparent overseas than they had been in my home country. I even discovered new weaknesses that I didn't know I had!

God does much in us before he can do much through us. Newcomers must be careful to come not just as movers and shakers, but as learners.

Together, we must be lifelong learners. We must be patient with each other, assertive when necessary, and most importantly (as has already been stated several times), communicate!

Good Ideas and Helpful Tools

From Survey Respondents:

> "Singles are given the opportunity to be treated as adults, not just old college students (for example, we are given the option to have roommates at trainings and retreats instead of automatically being put into roommate pairs), and are valued by the organization. Many people in the organization are single, both on the field and in the home office and administrative offices."

> "See each other as adults who have opportunity to offer hospitality to one another."

> "I guess, as being a single, my interaction/friendship with the kids/young adults is different yet encouraging, as I am not a parental figure but a different encouraging person (blessing?) in the lives of the kids. Also, being younger and independent, with different ideas, I think my team is encouraged by that, as I am encouraged by their perspective and experience."

Application Question

- What have you learned about maturity that will change future interactions with those younger or older than you?

CHAPTER 14

Expecting a Helping Hand and Not Always Finding One

STATEMENT

I do not get the help I need from others on my team due to my marital status.

MEAN
Married 1.15
Single 1.40

P-VALUE
.001

More single people than married people felt that they did not get the help they needed from their teammates because of their marital status.

There might be several reasons for this. In some cultures, it is difficult for men to help a single woman unless other people are around. Neighbors automatically assume immorality, especially among Westerners. At other times, husbands are busy with ministry and doing things for their wives and children; their time is limited. Single men might be willing to help, but may feel awkward if team members have been teasing about a possible future relationship with the single woman or if he is afraid the woman herself might take his help as a sign of interest in her.

Looking beyond culture, some wives are jealous. They can be fearful that their husbands might be tempted into an affair if they spend too much time with a single woman. They want their husbands at home with them; there are always things that need to be done around their homes and with their children.

Some of the respondents wrote about issues surrounding needed help and hindrances to receiving it, or reasons why it isn't offered:

"I feel like single people sometimes seem like a threat to 'family time' to one or both of a married couple."

"As a married person, I have special obligations to my wife and family that come above the needs of my other team members. That changes the dynamic completely."

"As a single woman, I have been denied rides after dark for the sake of propriety. It is also assumed, as a single, you can rearrange your schedule or accept whatever changes the marrieds/families need. I had to move out of my house to accommodate a family who lost their house, because I could move in with others. I overall feel very respected on my team, yet often I feel it is assumed that extra work is my responsibility as a single and that there is a double standard in expectations."

"Women are undervalued, ignored, and subservient in my host culture. Sometimes this means there are certain things it is better for a man to do than a woman. Single females might need a male team member to intervene. However, sometimes some single women forget that married men also have a family of their own and should not be demanding—[they] need to be sensitive to that."

Recently a teammate needed something repaired in her home. Don is handy, and he dropped by to help out. In the culture where we live now, that isn't a problem. When ministry is taking place in more conservative areas of the world, or with people who come from those places, it can a bit more difficult. Creativity is needed in how to help.

For instance, a single woman needed help from a married teammate to fix a broken sink in her apartment. His wife was out of the country. At this point in time the three of them were the only team members, and their three-way relationship was strong. People in their community saw them as family; it wasn't strange seeing any two of them together. The husband was viewed by the community as the protector/brother of his single teammate.

In order for him to help her, the three of them talked together using FaceTime while he was in her apartment fixing the sink. His wife knew he was there; the three of them talked together until he was finished and left. There was no hiding. If it came about when the wife returned that someone mentioned him going there, she could say, "Oh, I know. We were talking while he was there."

Trust has been built, and people know what their relationship is like. The married woman has also worked hard getting to know this single teammate, and they do things together. The couple talk about what is comfortable and what is not for them. The single woman also gives insight into what she needs and what her comfort level is. The end result is that she is helped. The married couple are aware and communicate often. They creatively find ways to be of help. Cultural norms are maintained.

Suzy shares a story of the dilemma of asking for help as well as giving it:

There can be pressures on the married couple and pressures for singles as these situations are navigated. Our best efforts to care for one another depend on how we're doing in our marriages or in our singleness. I remember a time when a couple I was working with had a lot of strain in their marriage. They were juggling a lot, the ministry was taking off, their children were young, and there were maintenance issues in their home. The wife was feeling like the husband wasn't doing all she hoped at their place. I needed some help with some repairs at my place too. I learned pretty quickly that it just put more strain on them to have yet another task added to the list.

If we're in a good place in our singleness, we understand that our teammates don't "owe us" and can't always help with every practical need. We want to lighten their load, too. That couple did get through that time and are some of the most generous people I know in caring for others outside their own family.

Some women are more handy than men, and some women are more handy than other women. I have depended on my husband to change out the water dispensers, take out the trash, and do home repairs. Other women do those things and do them well! Single women don't always need help nor want it! Valuing independence, they want to try things on their own, and they feel smothered if too much is done for them. Talking about these expectations or needs is essential for team relationships. We don't want to encourage dependency; we do want to be of service to others.

There have been a few times I've wrestled with jealousy when I've seen Don talking with a younger, single woman. This says more about me than him or her! I trust them both, but in my weakness and insecurity I've felt the sting of jealousy at times. I don't think I've ever tried to stop him from helping or talking with women; I've just battled the jealousy bug within, and thankfully it has never become a big issue. It really helps when I have a strong relationship with him and the other women on our team.

Years ago, when we were on a team with married and single people, I became sick and the doctors were trying to diagnose my illness. I am very seldom ill and tend to be melodramatic when I am. Because I wasn't feeling better quickly and it was taking a long time to figure out what was wrong with me, I became convinced that I was going to die. I didn't want to die! I wanted to see my children grow up. I wanted to meet my grandchildren.

I didn't want Don to marry anyone else—What if he ended up liking her more than me?

I had been praying for a husband for my single friend. Now I was afraid that the answer to my prayer would precipitate my own death. I would die, and the husband that I was asking for her would turn out to be mine! I stopped praying for a husband for her, since it seemed to coincide with my imminent departure from this world. I was never really jealous of her; I just thought they might get together.

I am thankful that I was eventually diagnosed and God healed me! I am also thankful that even though I had stopped praying for my friend to find a husband, she did; and I didn't have to die in the process. God led her to a husband, and I got to live and keep mine.

What is interesting is that when I was talking with some of the other married women on the team, I learned that they too thought that if something happened to them, their husbands would marry this single teammate! We loved her; she was great. We weren't jealous when we were living, but we thought we knew what would happen if we died!

As has already been alluded to in a previous chapter, as married couples we need to reevaluate how we view our single sisters and not suggest or even hint that they are threats to our marriages.

There are a few teammates who do not view their main role in ministry as being a help to their team. Some are task-oriented. Others see ministry to their national friends as more important than ministry to their team. They see danger when people want teams to replace families. For example, one man wrote,

> Things start getting out of whack when people look to make their ministry team to be their replacement family/family they never had/family that they wish they had or have. We are here to do a job primarily, not indulging ourselves in a mutual-care party, squeezing in occasional watercooler WWJD platitudes.

No one wants to move overseas just to do "team life" and forget about vision and ministry. Surely there is a place for helping each other, mutually caring for each other, and indeed doing what Jesus did for those in need!

Some people look to their team for their sense of community; others do not. Talking about it will help teams clarify expectations. The next chapter explores different expectations people might have of their team.

Good Ideas and Helpful Tools

Use the holidays to creatively lend a hand! Suzy shares this story:

> When I moved into my new apartment just before Christmas, I had lots of little tasks that needed to be done to make the place livable. But of course the month of December is already so busy, and the team had already helped me get the boxes from the old place to the new. But I knew it would be a while before I'd be able to get settled.
>
> At our field Christmas party we had drawn names and had to give gifts of time or service to the person whose name we had drawn. I opened an envelope and found a card that said, "I'll be your handyman—good for one day's work." This guy lived across town and was part of a different team—and actually loved working with tools. I jokingly said, "Can you come tomorrow?" He said, "Let me check with my wife."
>
> She was fine with it. He and one of his teenage daughters arrived the next morning to help me get all the electrical stuff wired, holes drilled, furniture put together, and pictures hung. Together we made a great team, and it got done quickly. I'd never been given such a practical and timely gift of help! I was grateful to God and this family for such a creative gift, too. It was just what I needed.

From Survey Respondents:

ONE MAN SHARED THAT BROTHERHOOD might look like going with a teammate to meet her fiancé as 'father stand-in' to make sure he was a decent guy and not a green-card seeker. It also means drinking innumerable coffees with guys who are green-card seekers and are pursuing our female teammates in entirely inappropriate ways and explaining again and again that 'no means no.' Blocking, bringing in national friends to try to convince these guys to lay off, etc."

I HAD FOUND THAT IT WAS HELPFUL to volunteer help. One of the ways I tried to make myself available was to ask during our one-on-ones if there was any help needed with the computer, with any 'around-the-house' things, etc. Anything that was stereotypically 'male' in its task, I tried to ask if there was a way to help. For many of these tasks, it was unnecessary to help; it was easy enough to call and hire a person to do it. But for some of these things, like computer maintenance, where it was unclear how trustworthy or skilled someone else was, it was considered a blessing to be of help (both for me and my teammate)."

[ONE] MARRIED COUPLE TRADED 'HELPS' with the single. [The husband] came and did handyman jobs, and the single picked up supper at a fast-food place on the way to team meetings."

Application Question

• What resources are necessary to see that those who need help receive it?

CHAPTER 15

Expecting More Time from Them When There Is Less Family

STATEMENT	MEAN
More community ministry time is expected from single people than married people on our team.	Married 1.70 Single 2.00 *P*-VALUE .006

Single people definitely felt that more ministry time is expected of them than those who are married. Is this merely the perception of singles, or is it a reality that they face? It could be that singles expect more from themselves and assume that others expect more as well. Because they don't have a spouse or children, they might think they should do more than their married teammates and that more is required of them by their organization. However, it could also be that organizations haven't tackled this topic in training. As a result, people are left to their own assumptions and expectations—and arrive on a team that already has its own assumptions and expectations!

We need to ask ourselves and our members if this is indeed an issue. If so, is it at the team level or does it stem from an organizational culture? Each organization needs to look at its policies and training to see what is being taught and where, if at all, this topic is addressed. If it is a field issue, leadership needs to ensure that it is proactively discussed before team members arrive, as well as after they arrive. If this view seems pervasive across all fields, then something is off-balance in the organization.

In his thesis, "Toward an Increased Effectiveness of Single Missionaries," Andy Smith writes:

> Many singles also discover that the careers given them on the field require great amounts of time and concentration. This commitment is also expected of their married teammates. The married missionaries, however, have a spouse to help them complete many of their tasks. So a single worker with the same career as a married person usually has to perform more duties. Many unmarried workers complain of unrealistic workloads because of this situation. (1988, 31)

Given the amount of time and concentration involved, it seems almost unavoidable that single workers would face a greater challenge keeping up with all that is required. Keep in mind how much longer it takes to complete the more mundane tasks of living like laundry, cooking, and shopping in many parts of the world where men and women serve. Without someone to help with those tasks—on top of language study, ministry opportunities, communicating with supporters, team meetings, financial reports, and so on—singles have many responsibilities to handle on their own.

A sister organization's member-care guide highlights this balance struggle for singles:

> Personal time versus ministry time is an especially important distinction for singles. It can be easy to assume that because they don't have families on the field, they can work longer, more flexible hours. They may be tempted to ensure their value in the team through overwork. Leaders might even be tempted to think the extra ministry time will somehow compensate for singles not having family. Keep in mind, though, that all housekeeping responsibilities remain, although no spouse is there to share the burden. (MTW Europe Member Care 2011, 2)

This struggle between personal time and ministry time is not just felt by singles, though. Married women, especially those with young children, also feel overwhelmed with balancing ministry in and outside of their homes. Even with help from their husbands, who are usually more involved in community ministry, they also struggle to contribute to ministry outside of their homes. At times, single teammates might not see the struggles the married women have because they assume the husband is helping. There are many husbands who do; there are also those who are so consumed with ministry outside of their homes that they forget the importance of their roles at home. The wives, who may also have part-time or full-time jobs and ministry opportunities, are left to handle the parenting and home side of ministry on their own.

Don dedicated time to his ministry in the home and fathering our children. I remember a marked difference in our family as he began to choose more intentionally to minister in our home and not just focus on the ministry outside of it. Balancing time in our spheres of ministry is not just a women's issue—men and women both have a vital ministry in the home. Choosing how much time to invest in each sphere of ministry is something about which mothers and fathers must be purposeful and prayerful. We talked about it together and made some adjustments, but were still never sure we were balancing well! It isn't easy to discern how to juggle all we need and want to do. We look back on the time we poured into ministering in our home as an eternally valuable investment of time and energy.

Married women have the advantages of freedom and flexibility that most mission agencies give them as they seek to juggle roles. As believers, we value the roles parents have in raising their children with love and a desire for godliness. I am so thankful for the way our mission supported me as a young mother and as a missionary.

I am afraid singles don't have that same freedom when it comes to all they need to do at home. Even without a spouse or children to care for, it is much more time-consuming to live cross-culturally. Married men can be out and about, and when they come home a meal might be ready and laundry might be done. This is never guaranteed, of course, but is often likely—depending on the day! If a married woman goes out and her husband is home, when she comes home it is possible that some of her tasks have been completed by her husband (if he is a wise husband). When a single person comes home after a full day of ministry, what was left undone is still there to do! Married couples can divide other responsibilities, such as visa applications, writing newsletters, and financial reporting. Singles are responsible to do all this on their own, as well.

In an interview, one single woman talked about having no excuse as a single person, so she expected herself to do more. She sees leadership giving more grace to moms with small kids. Everyone on her team is expected to do fifty to sixty hours of ministry each week, but more slack is given to women with kids. This feels unfair, and some seem to take advantage of the grace being offered. She said, "Different expectations are OK up to a point."

What is that point? How is it defined, and who defines it? What are our organizations' policies? Are they clear? Are they interpreted and practiced in different ways depending on the team and host culture?

I think everyone understands that there are different expectations. The confusion comes when there are differing opinions on what those expectations are or should be.

While I am thankful for the freedom given to me as a mother, I am wondering about something I don't remember thinking about until recently. What support and flexibility do organizations show their single members, as they also minister in and out of their homes?

Single men and women have homes. They have responsibilities outside of ministering in the community. They have extended family, deepening friendships, and home tasks that need to be done—as well as what they need to do to make their house a home. They also need to make time to rest, to have boundaries that protect their physical, spiritual, and emotional health. When we expect them to do more ministry than married members and ignore all that they still need to do outside of that, we are possibly being boundary-crashers who could contribute to burnout and the preventable attrition of our coworkers. When we take advantage of their strong work ethic and don't intervene when we see they are overstretching their limits, we are not being caring coworkers.

Suzy remembers a lesson the Lord taught her on rest:

> I've always struggled with really resting and almost "needing permission" when something in my schedule has to give. I remember one particularly busy month of ministry. I was fighting fatigue and a bad cold. But we had a field meeting that I didn't want to miss. As I dragged myself out of bed that morning, I felt sicker and sicker, but I pushed through and got to the field meeting. As we sat down to begin, I looked around the room and realized that almost all the other women were absent. As we went around the table, the men each mentioned why their wives weren't present. One was home with a sick child. One had a lot going on and her husband told her to stay home and rest. Another stayed in bed sick, and so on.

> As I sat there, I felt myself wishing that I would have had someone to tell me to stay in bed that day. That's when I realized it was my own pushing through—not anyone else's expectations—that had landed me at that meeting when I should have stayed home.

> Right then and there I asked the Lord to help me by telling me when I needed to take a break, cancel something, stay in bed, or say no to something else in my schedule. He has even run interference for me by having people cancel things when I needed a break in my schedule and didn't want to be the one to call things off. And he often whispers, "Are you sure you should take that on?" Or sometimes it's something like, "I want you home by XX time."

> I wish I could say that I always listen to that "still, small voice." But I'm getting better at discerning it, and I'm grateful for all the ways he is protecting me and truly being a husband to me in this process.

When asked "What hinders a good relationship between single and married people on a team?" survey respondents expressed varying perspectives regarding time and expectations:

"Single women can think married women with children don't do enough."

"Ignorance of each other's time management: Singles look at couples and families and see how they can share the load in many areas; marrieds look at the singles and see all the free time they have to do ministry, and fun things too."

"Married women expect single women to perform the same social duties as they do, while men expect them, at the same time, to do the same ministry duties."

"A lack of understanding [of] the others' lives and the temptation for people to compare themselves to others are the ones that come to mind immediately. Sometimes singles forget that married teammates have different personal responsibilities than singles do and cannot be as flexible with their time. Sometimes married teammates forget that the singles don't have anyone to help out with things their spouse does, so their expectations for the amount of free time a single has may be exaggerated."

This is an important topic not only for organizations to examine in their policies and training, but for teams to look at as well.

It seems that sometimes, in our desire to see the least-reached peoples of the world reached with the gospel, our organizational focus can be on "human doing," not necessarily on "human being." Peter Scazzero writes in *The Emotionally Healthy Leader* about the need for Sabbath rest and how hard it is to rest when we focus too much on the importance of what we do:

Part of who we are is what we do. God is a worker, and we are workers. But that is not the deepest truth about who we are. We are first of all human beings. But when things get switched around and our role or title becomes the foundation of our identity, we are reduced to human doings. And when that happens, ceasing work or productive activity becomes extremely difficult. (2015, 154)

How much ministry time are we expecting from Christian workers? Do we expect and require them to take days of rest and vacation time? Are singles at a disadvantage when needing time off for extended family challenges? Some single people felt more valued because of all they could do, not because of who they were. They sensed that others saw them as "workhorses" who could get a lot done.

Different people also have different capacities. A person with low energy will not accomplish the same number of things in a day as a person with high energy. But with wisdom, they choose their priorities and accomplish what is needed.

Discussions need to take place at organizational and team levels about expectations of and for each other. Too often we assume what others expect and we keep working to meet expectations that are perceived and not real. Teams should examine their true expectations and evaluate if any of them are unrealistic for those who are either married or single.

Good Ideas and Helpful Tools

From Survey Respondents:

One survey respondent suggested some ways teams should describe their expectations:

- Before going to the field, have each write their expectations of the other so they can identify what they think as an individual. (Sometimes we don't know what we think until we have to write or talk about it.)

- Talk about these role expectations with team leader before going to the field.

- Team leader or members on the field should communicate with appointees before their arrival to build relationship and talk through questions and expectations.

- Of course, more expectations will be realized upon arrival to the field, and an open atmosphere for questions and discussion is best related to this topic of roles and responsibilities of married and single people.

- Don't categorize single and married as different people groups. Focus on what you have in common, which is most everything.

Other respondents shared:

I THINK ONE SMALL THING that can mean so much is taking the time to express interest in the well-being of another. It's almost never the case that a husband on my team inquires after me, 'How are you doing with your new roommate?' 'Are things going well in your new office space?' 'What's your workload like nowadays?' 'Are things back home OK?' These questions and others go so far to make a person feel valued. These questions are not overly intimate and don't require some sort of close relationship to be asked. They simply confirm that 'You see me' and 'I am valued.' … And single women should feel valued by the men on their team."

[HAVE] DISCUSSIONS WITH THE TEAM on roles and expectations of each team member. We talked about the unique situations of each single and married member of the team—i.e., rather than just lump singles into one category, we looked at who they are and what their gifting was, and set roles and expectations accordingly. We did the same with married members (with and without children)."

"**SPEAK TO BOTH THE SINGLE AND THE MARRIED** about that [team] dynamic. And speak to both about putting unrealistic expectations on mothers, specifically with young children, as it relates to language learning, culture, ministry, and the timing of it all."

"**EACH MUST RESPECT THE OTHER.** Singles must understand that both spouses must be considered and children are a part of the mix. Many singles do not consider the children when planning events."

"**SPEND TIME DISCUSSING THE ISSUES** in an open environment. Share stories, thoughts, role-play, say the hard things."

"**MY LEADER IS MY HUSBAND,** and we have had two single women and a single man on our teams at different times. He is always explicit in discussing singleness and expectations with them, pre-field and regularly on the field. It's part of his field-integration program that a new team member spends the first year doing, and there is specific discussion in the team about interaction between marrieds [and singles]. Also, we share relevant articles on the subject as we read them. Keeping the issues on the table and keeping lines of communication open help."

Application Question

• How do you discern whether expectations are realistic or unrealistic?

SECTION THREE

The Challenge

We wonder when young people are called to go into cross-cultural ministry and parents are hesitant to let them go or even convince them not to, if perhaps the church is out of balance in our value of physical family over our spiritual one.

In these last few pages, we want to share the importance of releasing children, married or single, to follow God's call—and, in some instances, the importance of children releasing their parents as they are called overseas, leaving their adult children and grandchildren behind. However much we love our family, we are compelled to love Jesus more.

CHAPTER 16

Loving Family Well and God More

When we say goodbye to our physical families to share the gospel in far-flung corners of the world, we are showing our faith in Jesus and our belief that we have become his children and are part of his forever family.

When parents tearfully release their children to serve God far from home, they acknowledge, too, the eternal kingdom to which we now belong.

When grandparents leave their children and grandchildren to serve across cultures, the almost unbearable pain of separation pales in comparison to the worthiness of the name of Jesus and the glory that is to come.

In today's world, Christians place a high value on family. And so they should. We wonder, though, when young people are called to go into cross-cultural ministry and parents are hesitant to let them go or even convince them not to, if perhaps the church is out of balance in our value of physical family over our spiritual one. In these last few pages, Suzy and I want to share, first of all, our gratitude to our parents who released us to follow God's call when it meant loss for them but gain for the kingdom. We also want to share the importance of releasing children, married or single, to follow God's call—and, in some instances, the importance of children releasing their parents as they are called overseas, leaving their adult children and grandchildren behind. However much we love our family, we are compelled to love Jesus more.

Leaving a Legacy of Leaving (Sue)

To leave is not easy. Some say it is too hard. We've heard, "We could never do what you do."

Really? If God Almighty—the sovereign ruler and creator of all—called you, would you really say no to him?

We could never do what we do without the grace and power of God. I don't know how many times I've wanted to give up, go home, quit.

But God meets me there, and we keep going by his grace. I know what it is like to say goodbye as a daughter, and also as a mother and grandmother. It is heart-wrenching.

When we told my parents about being called to serve overseas, my mom said, "Don didn't mention this when he asked to marry you!" We didn't know then that God would call us there. My parents would have loved to have had us close by. But they released us and did not say no to God. They trusted in him, even though it was heartbreaking and hard.

When we first left to go overseas, my parents came to help us pack up and to say goodbye to us and three of their grandkids. I had never seen my dad cry until that day. Their youngest daughter was leaving and taking some of their grandkids to the Middle East. It would be several years before they saw us again. As I watched them pull out of the driveway, my tears flowed. I was still excited about moving forward and following God's call on my life. But I didn't know it would hurt so much.

I was not there when my grandpa died.

My parents weren't with me when their seventh grandchild was born.

They came to visit, and we went on home assignment; and through the years I thought saying goodbye would get easier with practice.

I was wrong.

In 2010, as Don and I were contemplating moving back overseas away from our children and grandchildren, I was grieving. It was one thing to go overseas with our family, and another thing to leave them and our adorable grandchildren behind. I remember being in church, singing songs of complete surrender to God's will, and tears would be flowing from my eyes as I thought about leaving our family on one continent and going to another.

Around that time, I was able to attend the baby dedication of our granddaughter Alivia. I couldn't stop crying as I realized anew that I would not be a part of her everyday life.

I thought of my grandma, recalling some of my fond memories of her—playing in her home, eating meals with her, spending New Year's Eve with her as my babysitter. Guilt assailed me as I thought about how, in comparison to her, I was going to be a worse grandma because I wouldn't be there for my grandchildren. I was ultimately afraid they would have no memories of me! I couldn't drop over to babysit them so that my kids could have a date night. There would be no games at my house, because there would be no house.

Fearful thoughts taunted my mind. What if my grandchildren don't know me? What if they turned away in fear when I came to visit? What kind of legacy can I leave when I am not with them? They will one day know that I willingly left them to move to another corner of the world. What would that communicate to them?

As I wrestled through the idea of leaving and being a terrible grandma, God broke through to my heart with the idea that I would not be a worse grandma— I would be a different one. They would have memories of me, but these memories wouldn't necessarily be location-specific.

They will be able to remember talking with us on Skype with blown kisses and virtual hugs. They will recall our visits to their house—picnics under the dining-room table, playing Your Car My Car, Go Fish, and hide-and-seek. Two of our grandchildren remember when they came to visit us in South Asia, as we helped at a slum school and saw the Taj Mahal together. One grandson still asks me to show him "his bed" where he slept when they visited us. God has graciously blessed us with more opportunities to connect with our grandchildren than I ever thought possible!

When overseas, I sometimes send pictures and emails. We try to send postcards from different countries of the world. At Christmas we send them a picture book that we make especially for them. We give them little souvenirs from foreign places during each visit so that they know we think of them as we travel. We sometimes text with our oldest granddaughter and enjoy those short conversations with her. We play Skype peekaboo with the younger ones.

We and our kids are intentional about staying connected. Our objective is to demonstrate love to our grandchildren so clearly that they will know, beyond a shadow of a doubt, that even though we are far away, we love them. A lot. Oodles. Bunches. To beyond the moon and back.

And love is the basis upon which a legacy of leaving is built. If we succeed in letting them know even a portion of how much we love them, I believe we are leaving them a legacy of leaving that translates into a legacy of loving. This legacy is one of completely loving them, but also loving Jesus *so much more* that we leave when he calls. We follow, even when it hurts. We obey, though the cost is steep. We know in our hearts—and desire our children and grandchildren to recognize fully as well—that Jesus Christ is worthy of such sacrifice.

It is a sacrifice to move far away from family. Sometimes Skype isn't enough. At times it actually amplifies the anguish of separation even more. When our granddaughter Penelope was born and we could only see her on Skype, I longed to hold her. I wanted to be there—not on another continent. As we ended the call, I started to cry and couldn't control the tears. I was missing so much!

When we do get to visit, I've found that saying goodbye doesn't get any easier. There are just more grandchildren to love and miss. Leaving is hard, and as my body flies to its next destination, it takes time for my breaking heart to catch up!

Not everyone is called to this sacrifice. Some grandparents stay in their home culture and live near their grandchildren. Many of these grandparents are leaving a lasting legacy, as they get to see their grandchildren often. They are seeking to influence this new generation for Christ and bless them spiritually as they live out the gospel in their communities. The grandchildren can see Jesus at work in and through the lives of their grandparents day in and day out.

There are other grandparents who stay in their home country, longing to be near their children and grandchildren. But God calls their children and grandchildren to leave to serve him, and these grandparents inherit a legacy of not only staying but feeling left behind. It could be that these grandparents feel the ache of their sacrifice most deeply. Sometimes they are unable to fully express their sorrow in the midst of the excited anticipation their children are feeling for what lies ahead of them in ministry. Both sacrifice. The grandparents, though, may feel it more keenly than their children as goodbyes are said.

I did not realize the costly sacrifice my own parents made when our young family left them to go overseas in ministry until about twenty-five years later! I had been so excited and determined to follow through on God's call that I didn't spend a lot of time listening to my mom's heart. Before we left she would talk about missing us, worrying about us, wanting to see her grandchildren grow up. I briefly acknowledged what she said, and felt some sadness myself, but almost always brushed it aside in my eagerness to move forward. Now I understand more fully what she was feeling.

In the Gospels, there were some disciples who wanted to follow Jesus, but he sent them back to their homes to tell people there about him. Others were working near their homes, and Jesus called them to leave and follow him. For those who wanted to go, to return home was a sacrifice. For those who wanted to stay where they were, leaving was a sacrifice. For the families left behind, saying goodbye was a sacrifice. But all obeyed because they knew Jesus was worth following. He was worthy of any sacrifice. He still is.

The legacy of leaving is one that points to Jesus as our treasure. He is the one we love most, and all else pales in comparison. One day God may call some of our grandchildren to leave their homes to serve him across cultures. May they count the cost and find that, although following Jesus is costly, he deserves nothing less than our wholehearted, loving obedience.

Whether we are grandparents who go, stay, or are left behind, may God use each one of us to live by faith and point to the eternal worthiness of Jesus.

That would indeed be a legacy worth leaving.

Leaving a Legacy of Surrendering (Suzy)

I saw my parents exercise faith and surrender in releasing me to go overseas. In fact, I've shared their example with many over the years. My parents' faith was a simple one. When I first went to the mission field, I would say they were nominal Christians. Even as nominal Christians, though, they told me frankly that they sensed God's hand in my life, stating their conviction that God had "set me apart." They dared not get in the way of God! They gave me their blessing to cross an ocean for cross-cultural service. All this, even though they didn't really understand the gospel deeply yet. As they came to know God more and appropriated the gospel for themselves, they were glad for my calling and delighted in watching him work.

My parents have faithfully prayed for me pretty much every day of the last thirty years I've been overseas. I was on home assignment earlier this year when my dad ended up in the hospital just days before I was to return to France. What began as treatable pneumonia turned into several other health issues. It became clear he wasn't going to recover. He begged us to take him home to die, believing this was his time; and the doctors finally agreed to release him to in-home hospice care.

As we loved on him the last week of his life, he couldn't wait to go to be with Jesus. Still, he worried about leaving us; he was such a protector and cared for his family. I assured him many times that the same one who would accompany him to heaven had promised to accompany us in the aftermath.

Throughout his life, my dad released me to answer God's call, even when he would have preferred to have me living closer. I think it was especially hard on him to let me leave as a single woman. He told me once he just wished there was someone taking care of me and he prayed for a husband for me. He never put any pressure on me to marry, but his father's heart wanted to be sure someone took his place to care for me. So my leaving meant his faith was tested, as was mine.

Accompanying Dad on his last earthly journey, I realized our roles had been reversed. As much as we would have loved to keep him with us just a little longer, it was his time to respond to a different call. I got to be on the other side of "releasing" him to die "in Christ" and travel home.

Through this tough time, both of my parents urged me to return quickly to France, and my mom willingly released me to leave the day after the funeral.

Though it cost us both, we had—and continue to have—a deep sense of God's peace. While I was praying just a couple of weeks later, the Lord whispered strong words of affirmation. The first was "We're really enjoying your dad!" Then he went on to say, "I will be your Father." At first I thought, "Well, of course you will; you've been my Father for a long time now." Then I realized he meant something else: that in the moments when I would miss my earthly father, he would be there for me. How comforting and precious were those words!

God has continued to be very close to my mom and me, and the rest of our family, during this time. For some parents, I think releasing their children into ministry feels like death. And having been released, and now asked to release, I can honestly say it's so worth it! We can't know God's grace, peace, the way he cares for us, and how he rewards those obedient to his call if we don't say yes.

The role of parents—Christian or not—is crucial. Being willing to release or willing to leave if God calls is how we live out our faith in obedience. But it is not without its own rewards. Remember the scene in the Gospels where Jesus and the disciples are talking about the sacrifices needed to enter the kingdom of God?

> As Jesus started on his way, a man ran up to him and fell on his knees before him. "Good teacher," he asked, "what must I do to inherit eternal life?"
>
> "Why do you call me good?" Jesus answered. "No one is good—except God alone. You know the commandments: 'You shall not murder, you shall not commit adultery, you shall not steal, you shall not give false testimony, you shall not defraud, honor your father and mother.'"
>
> "Teacher," he declared, "all these I have kept since I was a boy."
>
> Jesus looked at him and loved him. "One thing you lack," he said. "Go, sell everything you have and give to the poor, and you will have treasure in heaven. Then come, follow me."
>
> At this the man's face fell. He went away sad, because he had great wealth.
>
> Jesus looked around and said to his disciples, "How hard it is for the rich to enter the kingdom of God!"
>
> The disciples were amazed at his words. But Jesus said again, "Children, how hard it is to enter the kingdom of God! It is easier for a camel to go through the eye of a needle than for someone who is rich to enter the kingdom of God."

The disciples were even more amazed, and said to each other, "Who then can be saved?"

Jesus looked at them and said, "With man this is impossible, but not with God; all things are possible with God."

Then Peter spoke up, "We have left everything to follow you!"

"Truly I tell you," Jesus replied, "no one who has left home or brothers or sisters or mother or father or children or fields for me and the gospel will fail to receive a hundred times as much in this present age: homes, brothers, sisters, mothers, children and fields—along with persecutions—and in the age to come eternal life. (Mark 10:17-30)

Jesus tells us that when we leave for the sake of his kingdom, we will receive back—*in this present age*—a hundred times as much as we left. That's quite a return on our investment! I believe this is speaking of spiritual children, the new spiritual families that will be formed, and the sacred siblings that will join us in this journey—all because of our obedience in answering the call.

I recently celebrated thirty years in cross-cultural ministry. One of the privileges of the long haul is the fruit we get to see as God works slowly but surely in hard places. There is a panorama in my mind of precious faces of people who have come to embody the spiritual brothers, sisters, mothers, and children Jesus promised. They have made my journey, the hard times, and the cost of leaving rewarding. And that spiritual family has, in turn, blessed my physical family. These promises are real and continue to be offered as we work together to fulfill the Great Commission.

In conclusion, we are two women, one married and one single, whose parents released us to serve God. We can't help but think back to the New Testament and recognize two other sets of parents who released their unmarried sons to pursue their heavenly Father's will.

Zechariah and Elizabeth watched John the Baptist live counterculturally compared to other boys and young men his age. Maybe while they were playing ball, he was in the desert eating locusts. He dressed differently and lived differently as he followed where God led him. We're not sure how his parents fit in at the local parent-teacher meetings! But they knew God had called their son to ministry.

Mary and Joseph knew their son was unique. He truly was the Son of God as well as the Son of Man. By the time Jesus began his public ministry, his earthly father had almost certainly died. His mother watched as Jesus lived sinlessly, yet hung out with sinners. She watched him do miracles that made his life stand out;

and ultimately, because he is the way, the truth, and the life, sinners killed him. Mary grieved as she watched her son die a grievous and violent death at the hands of a mob. She might not have understood it fully, but she knew he was about his Father's business. His death brought life for many.

In this generation, may we follow in these parents' footsteps. May we joyfully, though sorrowfully, release those God calls to do his will around the world. And when he calls us, as tearful as we may be, may we gladly accept his call and go where he leads.

CHAPTER 17

Closing

Through our research we have discovered some significant differences in the perspectives of married and single missionaries in regard to their organizations, teams, and ministry expectations.

Our prayer is that after reading this book you will have discovered some practical ways to address some of these differences so that team relationships can thrive. As a result, ministries will flourish and people who trust in Jesus will know what it is like to be a beloved member of the family of God.

We also pray that this is the beginning of some helpful interaction between leadership and members, among team members, and between organizations. How can we share our resources for training? What can we do to help each other? As men and women, brothers and sisters, married and single people, we must consider how we are intentionally modeling sacred-sibling relationships.

For God's glory among the nations,
Sue and Suzy

APPENDIX 1

The Invitation

The Challenge of Mission in a Marriage Minority Culture

The New Reality ...

One of the most striking cultural shifts of the twenty-first century has been the sudden dramatic decline of marriage in the Western world. In the 28 EU nations, for example, from 1970 to 2010 the annual marriage rate has dropped almost 45%.[2] As a result, for the first time in modern history, many Western nations (including the UK, France, USA, Canada, and Australia) are now marriage minority cultures[3]— meaning that the majority of the adult population is single.

The situation in England serves as an illustration of the magnitude of this shift in the past century, where projections suggest that, within the next twenty years, almost 60% of the English adult population will be single.[4] Certainly, the cohabitation of unmarried adults has gained social acceptance as a valid alternative lifestyle and has been significantly on the rise in recent decades. But it is significant that the number of un-partnered single adults also continues to rise, with only the un-partnered singles projected to outnumber married adults in England and Wales in the next 20 years.[5] With some variation between countries, this trend is consistent across both Western and Eastern European nations.

---

2 The combined marriage rate for 28 EU countries has dropped from 7.9/1000 persons annually in 1970 to 4.4/1000 persons annually in 2010. This represents a decline of 44.3%. Source: Eurostat (www.ec.europa.eu/Eurostat), Marriage Indicators (demo_nind), Crude Marriage Rate, released May 30, 2016.

3 Based on marriage statistics for those of legal age to marry (usually 16 years and older). Singles outnumbered marrieds for the first time in the U.S. according to a report by economist Economist Dr. Edward Yardeni to *Bloomberg* on September 9, 2014 analyzing data from the U.S. Bureau of Labor and Statistics. Data for a wide spectrum of European countries is available online through the U.K. Office for National Statistics bulletin, Population estimates by Marital Status and Living Arrangements: England and Wales 2002 to 2014 released July 8, 2015. See page 13 for a table by European nation.

4 These projections are from the U.K. Office for National Statistics report, Population Trends 136, published in 2009, page 114.

5 Based on a recent U.K. ONS report no longer available.

The Internal Challenge...

What are the ramifications of this trend for the missions community of the twenty-first century? For those sending missionaries from Western countries, the implications are huge. As the proportion of singles increases in these missionary sending cultures at large, the pool from which new candidates are chosen will inevitably become increasingly single. Good stewardship of this new generation of workers will require that sending agencies be prepared to empower and leverage this valuable human resource—fully integrating them into every aspect of ministry, team, and leadership.

The External Challenge...

For those serving in Western countries, the new reality has huge implications for the world we are trying to reach. How can a church, emphasizing strong marriages and family values, avoid alienating the single culture just outside their door? Studies show that among the unreached or unchurched population, proportionately there are even more singles than in society at large. This means that if singles make up 50–55% of adult society, they typically represent 60-70% of the unreached people in that same society.[6] It is easy to imagine how these unchurched singles could feel excluded from churches that are well-meaning but unprepared. Having healthy and able singles fully functioning within our mission teams will be vital in bringing the gospel to the large and growing population of singles in these cultures.

It is painfully obvious that the decline of marriage in society has been accompanied by an exponential rise in other challenges. We are bringing the gospel to a different kind of world! In doing so, we must be prepared to speak effectively into the experiences of same sex attraction and marriage, transgender and gender dysphoria, alternative sexualities, sexual addictions, pornography, and divorce. All of these challenges require a biblical response that is not merely reactionary to culture, but is also constructive and deeply rooted in the ethos of the Scriptures.

---

6 See the Pew Research Study, "Nones" on the Rise: One-in-Five Adults Have No Religious Affiliation, released October 9, 2012 (www.pewforum. org/2012/10/09/nones-on-the-rise/), page 39.

Biblical Foundation...

As Christians, we acknowledge that the starting point for responding to cultural issues is God's Word; and we know the Bible affirms a high view of marriage, family, and human sexuality. Interestingly, Christianity shares these values with other religions including Judaism, Islam, and Mormonism. But while all these faiths affirm a high view of marriage and human sexuality, Christianity is unique in also teaching a high view of singleness.

This distinction is not accidental but fundamental to the gospel message we proclaim. Under the Old Testament, God's blessing was expressed through marrying and having physical children. Barrenness and singleness were regarded as unblessed states of reproach and disgrace. But in the New Testament, Jesus Christ alone is the fulfillment of all spiritual blessings. Awareness of this unfolding of the whole of Scripture provides the basis for understanding why singleness is affirmed in the New Testament, both by the teachings of Jesus and through the inspired writings of Paul. But even more than this, it provides the basis for understanding the reality of the new spiritual family we have in Christ and the nature of how singles and marrieds are intended to work together in producing spiritual offspring in the kingdom of God.

Shoulder to Shoulder ...

Solid biblical theology leads to sound practical theology in living out the new reality of who we are in Christ, as we serve on teams in mission together. This involves effectively leveraging all individuals, be they single or married, with or without children, as fully complete in Christ, and uniquely equipped members of our mission teams. It also entails understanding the unique challenges singles and marrieds both face working together as teams in the body of Christ.

Shoulder to Shoulder exists to come along-side cross-cultural workers, mission teams, and organizations with resources and supportive community to prepare them for the new realities and challenges of effective cross-cultural life and ministry—equipping them to integrate and empower every member.

Our team is available to offer consultation and training, as well as a range of resources available through the web site www.ShouldertoShoulder.global. Together we can be prepared to face our changing world, as we share the gospel cross-culturally through the twenty-first century and beyond.

DR. BARRY N. DANYLAK, with contributions from DR. ROBERT D. LUGAR

Shoulder to Shoulder

Empowering. Equipping. Encouraging.

"So that all may serve the Lord shoulder to shoulder." —ZEPHANIAH 3:9

www.shouldertoshoulder.global

An Initiative of One Another Ministries
s2s@oneanother.com

APPENDIX 2

The Letter

11/23/16

Dear Co-Laborers,

My name is Sue Eenigenburg. I have been involved in cross-cultural ministry for over thirty years. I am currently the director of women's ministry in Christar, a church planting mission organization.

I have recently begun researching relationship issues among married and single people working together on teams. I began by looking for resources already available about this topic. I found material for those who are single missionaries. I found material for those who are married in missions. I discovered very little written about team dynamics among married and single people working together in ministry teams. In the last few years I have had opportunities to listen to single and married people talk about some of the team issues they face because of their mixed marital statuses. We all need to grow in our awareness of what some of these issues are and to develop intentional and creative ways to address them. This can help our teams be more effective in modeling the spiritual family the body of Christ was designed to be, and may in fact help lower attrition rates.

In order to learn more, I would like to send out a survey to help identify challenges facing married and single persons working together in cross-cultural ministry teams and to discover factors that would enhance healthy team relationships.

The overarching goal is to help organizations, leaders and teams get a realistic picture of what some of the issues are that mixed marital status teams face. We should also discover how organizations can improve orientation and training for these teams. Another outcome is to gain as well as examine ideas that might prove helpful to teams to understand and work well with each other. There is a plan to write about the survey results so that we all learn how team relationships can flourish and team ministries can grow in fruitfulness. Suzy Grumelot, a member of World Team with rich ministry experience, will join me in this venture.

This survey is to be sent to teams who have had or currently have married and single people working together. Each person on the team is to complete the survey, including the team leader.

If your mission agency is willing to participate by sending the survey to your mixed-marital status teams, please let me know by December 31. I plan to begin sending out the survey at the beginning of next year. Please let me know who to send the survey link to so it could then be forwarded to the appropriate teams.

To be of service and to thank you for encouraging members in your agency to participate, I would be happy to provide a short summary specific to results pertaining to your organization.

Let me know if you have any questions or concerns. I hope that your agency will be a partner in this research endeavor. I look forward to hearing from you before December 31, 2016.

Sincerely,
Sue Eenigenburg

APPENDIX 3

The Survey

Goal of this survey

To identify challenges facing married and single persons working in cross-cultural ministry teams and to discover factors that would enhance these team relationships.

Recipients of this survey

This survey is to be sent only to teams who have had or currently have married and single people working together. Each person on the team is to complete the survey, including the team leader.

Data

Gender _____

Age _____

Marital Status

Married __ Never married __ Divorced __ Widowed __ Remarried __

Organization _____

How many years have you served in cross-cultural ministry? _____

What is your current ministry role? _____

_____

What people group are you serving _____

My home country _____

My team makeup

Number of: married couples ___, single men ___, single women ___

Questions

If a question below does not apply to you, use the number 0 for not applicable. Otherwise, please insert number in the blank that most closely aligns with your opinion:

0 Not Applicable   1 Rarely   2 Sometimes   3 Often   4 Always

____ 1. My organization values single and married people equally.

____ 2. Pre-field training in my organization intentionally prepares singles for missions.

____ 3. Pre-field training in my organization intentionally prepares married couples for missions.

____ 4. Pre-field training in my organization intentionally prepares married and single people to work together on teams in missions.

____ 5. I feel supported by my team.

____ 6. My team knows my needs and seeks to meet them.

____ 7. My team leader values me and my contribution to ministry.

____ 8. The opinions of single women and married women are equally valued.

____ 9. Single women's opinions are respected more than those of married women on our team.

____ 10. Single men tend to be more alienated from team life than single women.

____ 11. My team leader solicits my input.

____ 12. I feel unwanted by my team.

____ 13. I am not needed on my team.

____ 14. I seek to meet needs of others on my team.

____ 15. The host culture I am in respects women regardless of their marital status.

____ 16. There is good communication between married and single people on my team.

____ 17. I have a way to process information after team meetings or from mission leadership.

____ 18. Leadership in my organization values my opinions.

____ 19. Leadership in my organization requests my feedback on important issues.

____ 20. I sense that my team leader understands me.

____ 21. I am seen as a perceived threat to the marriages of couples on my team.

____ 22. I trust my team leader.

____ 23. I am trusted by my team.

____ 24. My host culture's view of women negatively influences my team in how women are treated.

____ 25. Women are seen as sisters in Christ by the men on my team.

____ 26. I am content in my current marital status.

___ 27. I take time to listen to each member of my team.

___ 28. I thought my team would be like a family, but it does not provide the community I need.

___ 29. I have found my community outside of my team and am content with it.

___ 30. I am seen as a little sister or little brother on my team who is not treated like an adult.

___ 31. I do not get the help I need from others on my team due to my marital status.

___ 32. The idea of my team being a spiritual family appeals to me.

___ 33. I am eager to share my views with leadership because my input is appreciated.

___ 34. I am encouraged to use my spiritual gifts and feel fully utilized in ministry.

___ 35. More community ministry time is expected from single people than married people on our team.

___ 36. Singles have freedom to determine their own housing situation in our organization.

___ 37. I have considered leaving my organization due to issues involving their treatment of me based on my marital status.

Please give brief answers to the following questions:

1. How did your organization specifically prepare you for team life with married and single people working together?

2. What suggestions do you have that would prepare missionaries of mixed marital statuses to work well together on teams?

3. How does leadership in your organization view singles?

4. Does gender or marital status influence ministry opportunities in your organization? Please explain.

5. Does gender or marital status influence ministry opportunities in your host culture? Please explain.

6. What hinders a good relationship between single and married people on a team?

7. What do people of different marital statuses need to know in order to provide a sense of community for each other?

8. How does one's marital status influence team relationships?

9. How does your host culture's view of singleness influence your team's view of singles?

10. What can men and women coworkers do to develop healthy relationships?

11. Please share examples of how your marital status has impacted relationships on your team.

12. If you have any other insights that you would like to share, please do.

References

Books

Clarkson, Margaret. 1978. *So You're Single! Margaret Clarkson Reflects on Singleness.* Wheaton, IL: Harold Shaw.

Danylak, Barry. 2010. *Redeeming Singleness: How the Storyline of Scripture Affirms the Single Life.* Wheaton, IL: Crossway.

Edwards, Sue. 2008. *Mixed Ministry: Working Together as Brothers and Sisters in an Oversexed Society.* Grand Rapids: Kregel.

Hawker, Debbie, and Tim Herbert, eds. 2013. *Single Mission.* Fresno, CA: Condeopress.

Lockerbie Stephenson, Jeannie. 2008. *By Ones and Twos: Building Successful Relationships between Marrieds and Singles in Ministry.* Harrisburg, PA: ABWE Publishing.

O'Malley, Ed, Julia Fabris McBride, and Amy Nichols. 2014. *For the Common Good: Participant Handbook.* Wichita: Kansas Leadership Center.

Ortberg, John. 2001. *If You Want to Walk on Water, You've Got to Get Out of the Boat.* Grand Rapids: Zondervan.

Scazzero, Peter. 2015. *The Emotionally Healthy Leader: How Transforming Your Inner Life Will Deeply Transform Your Church, Team, and the World.* Grand Rapids: Zondervan.

Smith, Marti. 2004. *Through Her Eyes: Perspectives on Life from Christian Women Serving in the Muslim World.* Downers Grove, IL: InterVarsity Press.

Documents

Danylak, Barry. 2006. "A Biblical-Theological Perspective on Singleness." http://www.hantla.com/blog/images/biblical_singleness.pdf.

MTW Europe Member Care. 2011. "The Benefits and Care of Single Missionaries." April 5, https://www.mtwcare.org/uploads/8/9/8/6/89863841/the_benefits_and_care_of_singlemissionaries_e.pdf.

Smith, Andy P. 1988. "Toward an Increased Effectiveness of Single Missionaries." Unpublished thesis.

Online Resources

Becker, Joshua. "The Unmistakable Freedom of Contentment and How to Find It." *Becoming Minimalist,* https://www.becomingminimalist.com/the-unmistakable-freedom-of-contentment-and-how-to-achieve-it/.

Cleveland, Christena. 2018. "Six Tips on How Married Christians Can Embrace Single Adults." *The Andy Gill Blog,* March 7, http://www.patheos.com/blogs/andygill/6-tips-on-how-married-christians-can-embrace-single-adults/.

Eenigenburg, Sue. 2017. "When Harassment Meets Forgiveness." *Screams in the Desert Blog,* December 5, https://screamsinthedesert.wordpress.com/2017/12/05/when-harassment-meets-forgiveness/.

Graybill, Ruth Ann. "The Emotional Needs of Women on the Mission Field." Posted on *Living Hands Network,* March 8, 2010, http://en.liftinghands.net/selfstudy_detail.php?a=3&b=8&t=20.

Jenkins, Bethany. 2016. "Turning 40 While Single and Childless." *The Gospel Coalition,* October 5, https://www.thegospelcoalition.org/article/turning-40-while-single-and-childless/.

Lencioni, Patrick. "Communication Needs to 'Cascade' from Executive Suite." *The Table Group,* https://www.tablegroup.com/newsroom/news/communication-needs-to-cascade-from-executive-suite.

McCaulley, Esau. 2018. "It's Not My Daughter's Job to Teach Me About Women." *Christianity Today,* June 21, https://www.christianitytoday.com/women/2018/june/its-not-my-daughters-job-to-teach-me-about-women-kanye-west.html.

McHugh, Brent. 2018. "In the Know About Changes Ahead." https://imiconnect.wordpress.com/2018/04/20/in-the-know-about-changes-ahead/.

Rumsey, Deborah J. "What a *P*-Value Tells You about Statistical Data." *Dummies,* https://www.dummies.com/education/math/statistics/what-a-p-value-tells-you-about-statistical-data/.

Schilling, Diane. 2012. "Ten Steps to Effective Listening." *Forbes,* November 9, https://www.forbes.com/sites/womensmedia/2012/11/09/10-steps-to-effective-listening/#81eaf8f38918.

Till, Aidan. 2018. "Family Plus." *Revive* 49 (1), https://issuu.com/revivemagazine/docs/2018_singleness_revive_web?e=2326932/59591385.

Resources

To read the article on "The Call" by Keith Green: http://lastdaysministries.org/Groups/1000086194/Last_Days_Ministries/Articles/By_Keith_Green/Why_YOU_Should/Why_YOU_Should.aspx.

To read or listen to the sermon John Piper preached on April 29, 2007: http://www.desiringgod.org/messages/single-in-christ-a-name-better-than-sons-and-daughters.

To get a copy of Barry Danylak's original twenty-page work, "A Biblical Theology of Singleness," go to: https://grovebooks.co.uk/products/b-45-a-biblical-theology-of-singleness.

Other titles to consider:

By: Sue Eenigenburg and Robynn Bliss

Missionary women have high expectations when they respond to God's call; of themselves, their mission agencies, host cultures, churches, co-workers, and even of God. These expectations are often impossible to fulfill and can lead to mental and physical exhaustion. In *Expectations and Burnout: Women Surviving the Great Commission*, Sue provides research and surveys from the field while Robynn lends her own personal experiences to demonstrate how burnout can happen and how God can bring life from ashes.

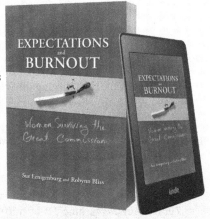

Buy now at
missionbooks.org.

I am grateful for the opportunity, through this book, to engage with my heavenly Father about my commitment to His mission to take the good news of Jesus to a lost world—no matter the risk, the hardship, the suffering, the tears. I am also thankful that I now have a much greater understanding of what the missionary mums that I regularly partner with in prayer are experiencing on the field.

—Lesley Ramsey
editor of *What Women Really Need*

Available at missionbooks.org

CPSIA information can be obtained
at www.ICGtesting.com
Printed in the USA
BVHW091351190922
647171BV00004B/7